Perfect Wedding Speeches and Toasts

George Davidson is a former senior editor with Chambers Harrap. He is an experienced researcher and writer of reference books and has participated in several weddings as bridegroom, best man, and father of the bride. He lives in Edinburgh.

Other titles in the *Perfect* series

Perfect
Wedding Speeches and Toasts

George Davidson

BOOKS

Published by Random House Books 2007

2 4 6 8 10 9 7 5 3

Copyright © George Davidson 2007

George Davidson has asserted his right under the Copyright, Designs
and Patents Act 1988 to be identified as the author of this work

First published in the United Kingdom in 2007 by
Random House Books

Random House Books
Random House, 20 Vauxhall Bridge Road,
London SW1V 2SA

www.randomhouse.co.uk

Addresses for companies within The Random House Group Limited
can be found at: www.randomhouse.co.uk/offices.htm

The Random House Group Limited Reg. No. 954009

A CIP catalogue record for this book
is available from the British Library

ISBN 9781905211777

The Random House Group Limited makes every effort to ensure that the
papers used in its books are made from trees that have been legally sourced
from well-managed and credibly certified forests. Our paper procurement
policy can be found at: www.randomhouse.co.uk/paper.htm

Typeset by Palimpsest Book Production Limited, Grangemouth, Stirlingshire
Printed in the UK by CPI Bookmarque, Croydon, CR0 4TD

Contents

Acknowledgements

The author would like to thank Sophie Lazar, Emily Rhodes and Sophie Hutton-Squire for their helpful comments on earlier drafts of this book, the Rev. John Davidson for his useful suggestions and advice, and David Foster for one particularly good idea.

Acknowledgments

Introduction

For some people, the thought of having to make a speech at a wedding reception is slightly daunting, or even (if they are totally honest) absolutely terrifying. They have never spoken in public before and have no desire whatsoever to do so, but they know that, thanks to their role in a forthcoming wedding, they are going to have to.

Others, while never having made a speech in public before, are not in the least daunted by it, and in fact are rather looking forward to it, but want to make sure that they do the job properly. They may not be entirely sure what they are going to say – or even what they are *expected* to say.

Others again, perhaps not inexperienced public speakers, have never proposed a toast at a wedding before, and like those in the second group above, want to make sure that they get it right.

And lastly, there may be some who would quite like to say something at a forthcoming wedding, but are not sure whether it would be the 'done thing' for them to do so. They know that by tradition the father of the bride, the bridegroom, and the best man make speeches and propose toasts, but would it be all right for someone else to speak as well?

Whatever category you belong to – experienced speaker or complete novice, daunted or undaunted, compelled to speak or hoping to speak – this book can certainly help you. It contains all the information about what to say and how to say it, taking you step by step through the whole process of planning, writing, rehearsing and delivering a perfect wedding speech and an appropriate toast to go with it.

Chapter one discusses who usually makes a speech at a wedding, and how to handle exceptional circumstances.

Chapter two describes the role of a master/mistress of ceremonies.

Chapter three provides some suitable graces that can be said before the meal (if required).

Chapters four, five, and six tell you how to prepare and write a speech, and how to practise and deliver it.

Chapters seven to eleven outline the contents of the various wedding speeches, both what *must* be said and what *may* be said in addition, with sample material that you can, if you want, use or adapt for your own speech.

Finally, in the Quick Reference section, you will find a wealth of material that you can use to embellish and enliven any speech.

Throughout the book, there are troubleshooting panels that suggest ways of avoiding or dealing with specific problems that could arise.

Some reassurance for the nervous ...

If you *are* worrying about making a speech, remember these three things:

- No one is expecting you to be a brilliant, polished, professional after-dinner speaker (unless, of course, you are!). You don't need to try – in fact you really *shouldn't* try – to impress your listeners by being something you aren't. Just be yourself. Be natural.

- You will be among friends, so be relaxed about your speech. Everyone else will be. No one will be out to criticise you, unless you give them something to criticise (which means you must avoid inappropriate remarks and jokes that some people might consider to be in poor taste).

- Your speech should probably not last more than a few minutes. The time will pass very quickly when you are speaking, and you will find that you won't need a lot of speech to fill four (or even just two or three) minutes.

Remember: **the less you worry about your speech, the better it will be on the day.** You'll be more at ease, and seeing that you're at ease, your audience will be too. They will enjoy listening to you, and who knows, you *may* even surprise yourself and enjoy entertaining them!

How to use this book

Throughout this book, you will find many suggestions for what to say in your speech. But remember, **the best parts of your speech will be the parts this book cannot write for you – the parts that are personal to you and particularly apt for the occasion.**

The wedding you will be speaking at will be unique, your audience will be unique, and your speech must be unique, too. You will never produce a good wedding speech by simply parroting someone else's work; but by studying and adapting the suggestions, hints and samples in this book, you will be able to write for yourself a perfect wedding speech and toast.

No matter which speech you are making, you would be well advised to read through the whole book, as some of the suggestions made in the chapter on, say, the bridegroom's speech might equally be used by, for example, the best man. (But do check that you are not both going to use the same jokes and stories!)

Different traditions

Throughout this book, the focus is on weddings within the British Christian and secular traditions. Other religious, racial and cultural groups have, of course, their own wedding traditions.

If you are to speak at a wedding being carried out within a different cultural tradition from your own, it is important that you find out early on what is expected of you, certainly before you start writing your speech.

The nature and content of your speech may not exactly match that of any of those described in this book, nor may the order of the speeches be the same as described here. However, the guidance given in this book on how to write and deliver a speech will still apply to your situation, and you will be able to adopt, or adapt, many of the suggestions given in chapters four to eleven.

1 Who makes a speech, what do they say, and when do they say it?

We will assume for the time being that this is going to be a fairly traditional wedding and wedding reception. (We will deal with variations later on.) We will, therefore, assume that there will be a bride and a groom, two sets of parents (with no divorces or bereavements), a male best man, and at least one bridesmaid or matron of honour.[1] The reception will be a sit-down meal, and it is the father of the bride who will be hosting it (and paying for it!).

In chapters seven to eleven we will cover both the necessary and the possible contents of the various speeches in detail, but at this point it will be useful to get an overview of the purpose of the main wedding speeches and how they relate to one another, so that you can see how your speech fits in to the whole system of things.

The toasts and replies

Typically, the speeches and toasts come *after* the meal and *before* the cutting of the wedding cake. There are three speeches, because you need three speakers to cover the two toasts that are traditionally made (there can be others, as we will discuss later in this chapter) and the two replies

[1] A matron of honour is a married bridesmaid. For convenience, throughout this book, where we talk about 'the bridesmaid', this should be understood to mean 'one or more bridesmaids or matrons of honour', and of course there may be one or more pageboys and flower girls too.

to these toasts. And by tradition the three speakers are the bride's father, the bridegroom, and the best man (in that order):

- The bride's father concludes his speech with a toast to the bride and groom.

- The groom begins his speech by thanking the bride's father for his kind words . . .

   . . . and concludes his speech with a toast to the bridesmaid.

- The best man thanks the bridegroom on behalf of the bridesmaid.

That is the basic structure of the toasts and replies. Anything else – any other thank yous, any jokes or anecdotes, etc. – is fitted into this framework.

Now the first thing to be noted is that there is, in fact, no necessity for anyone to make a speech at all. The father of the bride could simply stand up and invite everyone to join him in a toast to the bride and groom, in words along the lines of:

> *Ladies and gentlemen,*
>   *I would like you all to join me now in wishing John and Julie a*
> *very happy marriage.*
> [Turn towards the bride and bridegroom] *John and Julie.*

The families and guests would all stand, turn to the newly-weds, raise their glasses, repeat 'John and Julie', and sit down again. The bridegroom would then stand, thank his father-in-law for his good wishes and propose a simple toast to the bridesmaid, again joined by the families and the guests. The best man would stand, thank the bridegroom on behalf of the bridesmaid, and then read out the cards and letters of good wishes from people who have not been invited or not been able to attend the wedding.

At its simplest, that is all that is strictly required of the three speakers. And there could be good reasons why the bride and groom and their families might decide that this is all that will be said at the reception. But it's not very interesting, is it? Not much fun. Not very memorable. The toasts and replies are only the barest of bare bones – it's the speeches that go with them that add the fun and the interest on the day. So let's look (only briefly at this stage) at the contents of the three speeches.

The speeches

The father of the bride

The father of the bride, and as such the host at the wedding reception, should begin his speech by welcoming his guests and thanking them for coming. His speech should probably include the following:

- how proud he and his wife are of their daughter, and congratulations to the groom on his choice of wife

- an amusing or interesting anecdote or two about events in his daughter's life

- a few complimentary words about the groom, and how happy he and his wife are that their daughter has chosen such a fine husband

- his and his family's pleasure at meeting and getting to know the groom's family

- an amusing anecodote about something that happened during the wedding preparations, and/or a joke or two, or an amusing story

Finally he will bring his speech to a close by inviting everyone present to join him in his toast to the bride and groom.

The bridegroom

The bridegroom speaks mostly on behalf of his wife and himself, but of course, if talking to or about his bride, he is speaking for himself alone.

The easiest way for the groom to begin his speech is by thanking his father-in-law for his kind words and the toast. This both links his speech to what has gone before and also provides a lead-in to what he should say next. But of course he may want to begin his speech in some other way and bring in the thanks later on. The bridegroom's speech could include the following:

- thanks to the bride's parents for welcoming him into the family and allowing him to marry their daughter

- thanks to the bride's father for the wedding and the reception (perhaps also adding his thanks to the caterers, if they deserve it)

- thanks to his new wife for agreeing to marry him, and how fortunate he is to have such a beautiful/intelligent/successful/understanding/loving bride

- thanks to his own parents for how they have brought him up, and for their support and guidance through the years

- thanks to the guests for attending the wedding, for their good wishes, and for their gifts

- thanks to the best man and the ushers for their help and support

- thanks on his wife's behalf to the bridesmaid for her help and support

As you will have seen, a large part of the bridegroom's speech involves saying thank you, but just as with the father of the bride's speech, there should be some lighter moments. The bridegroom should probably include some information about how he and his wife met, perhaps with an amusing anecdote about how their relationship developed (or didn't at first!). There could also be an amusing story about something that happened during the wedding preparations.

Lastly, the bridegroom's speech should return to the bridesmaid. He has already thanked her for her help on behalf of his wife; now it is his turn to make some complimentary remarks about her, before inviting everyone to join him in a toast to her.

The best man

Although the best man's speech is usually more light-hearted than the previous two speeches – not that they should be in any way solemn – and focused to a great extent on the groom, with amusing stories about his past, his character, his foibles, etc., the best man does also have certain thank yous to make.

The following are the main elements of the best man's speech:

- He replies on behalf of the bridesmaid to the toast made by the bridegroom at the end of his speech.

- He acknowledges the groom's thanks to him and the ushers.

- He may, on his own behalf and on behalf of the guests, thank the bride's parents for the reception.

- He congratulates the bride and groom, expressing his good wishes for their future happiness, and of course makes some complimentary remarks about the lovely bride and the groom's good luck in persuading her to marry him.

At the end of his speech, the best man reads out the messages from well-wishers who are not at the wedding.

A key point to note is that **the best man does *not* toast the bride and groom** (a common mistake). The toast to the bride and groom has already been proposed by the father of the bride. The best man may not propose any toast at all, but he *may* be asked by the bride and groom to propose some other toast (which we will discuss in chapter ten).

That covers, in enough detail for the moment, the three main speeches of a traditional wedding reception. But of course not all weddings follow the traditional pattern. There may be more than three speakers, there may be fewer than three speakers, and there may be different speakers. We will consider each of these situations in turn.

More than three speakers

In the past, it was relatively rare for anyone other than the father of the bride, the bridegroom, and the best man to make a speech at a wedding. But things have changed. It is nowadays not uncommon for the bride to make a speech as well as the bridegroom (or jointly with the bridegroom, or even in some cases *instead* of the bridegroom); the bridesmaid may want to speak on her own behalf rather than having the best man express her thanks for her; and the bride's mother and either or both of the bridegroom's parents may also want to say something. A brother or sister may want to speak, as may the bride's or groom's children at, for example, a second wedding. And in addition there may be other members or friends of the families who have something they would like to say.

There is nothing against this. There is no necessary restriction to the number of speeches that can be made at a wedding, but one should always keep the guests in mind: listening to three speeches is fine, listening to four or five tolerable, but after that . . . well, there are limits! When does the dancing start?

The more speeches there are, the shorter they should probably be, and great care should be taken by all concerned that there is no unnecessary duplication or repetition. Anyone, other than the three traditional speakers, who plans to make a speech must have a clear idea of *why* they want to speak and in what way their words will contribute to the occasion.

Speeches by the bride, the bridesmaid, the father of the groom, etc. will be discussed in chapters ten and eleven. Here we will consider some other possible scenarios.

Two (or more!) best men

It is not uncommon nowadays for there to be two best men at a wedding. In that case, it is up to the two of them to discuss their roles with each other and with the groom and come to an agreement about who is to be responsible for what. One option is that one could make the best man's speech while the other acts as master of ceremonies at the reception and/or reads out the well-wishers' letters and cards.

If both best men want to speak, however (for example, because they each know the best man in different contexts or from different periods of his life), the speeches need to be carefully thought out – and, again, not too long. If they are speaking in turn, one way of arranging it would be as follows: the first speaker could cover the basic polite elements of the traditional best man's speech – thanks on behalf of the bridesmaid, thanks to the ushers on behalf of both best men, etc. – before contributing his anecdotes and jokes; he would then introduce the second best man, 'who would also like to say a few words about the groom'. The second speaker then contributes his own anecdotes. The two speakers should make sure to check that they are not intending to tell the same or very similar anecdotes or use the same jokes. When it comes to the reading of the cards and letters, either or both of them could do it, in any way agreed on in advance.

If there are more than two best men (it's possible), the same applies as when there are only two. It's just a question of planning the speeches carefully and agreeing on who is going to say what.

If the best men have time and inclination, of course, they could write the best man's speech together, integrating each of their contributions into a single speech. At the reception they would stand up at the same time, whether or not beside each other, and bounce the speech back and forth from one to the other. If well rehearsed and well performed, this could be very entertaining.

The double wedding

At a double wedding, such as the marriages of two sisters at the same ceremony, there are already a lot of 'main players' who will have to speak at the reception: one father of the brides, two bridegrooms and (at least) two best men. Possibly the two brides will also wish to say something. Under these circumstances, it would be wise if the bridesmaids allowed the best men to speak on their behalf (as is traditional), and other people were discouraged from speaking at all.

The key problem is the order of the speeches. One possible approach is as follows:

- The father of the two brides speaks first, as is normal, his speech taking in both brides, both bridegrooms, and both of the bridegroom's families.

- The new husband of the elder daughter speaks next, followed by his best man and then his bride (if she wishes to).

- Then the younger daughter's husband speaks, followed by his best man and his bride (if she wishes to).

- The best men should then read out the well-wishers' messages (shared between them according to which marriage or family the messages relate to, or any other way they choose).

An alternative solution would be for the two brides to speak after the well-wishers' messages have been read out, and to add some originality, they could make a joint speech in much the same way as was suggested for two best men to do in the section above.

Fewer than three speakers

Under what circumstances might there be fewer than the three 'traditional' speeches? Clearly, when there aren't enough people present to make three speeches, but also when the gathering is so small or so informal that three speeches would really not be wanted. (Remember that you can have toasts without speeches, and the only toast that is really required, regardless of the circumstances, is the one to the bride and groom.) In other cases, it might be that particular circumstances make it difficult or inappropriate to have all three speeches.

The key thing is for no one to feel *obliged* to have three speeches at a wedding meal. Tradition is fine, but it should not be a straitjacket.

The small wedding

If the wedding is held at a registry office, there may be no one present who has the role of best man. Although there will be a best man at a traditional religious ceremony, it is not a legal requirement that there be one at a civil marriage. The only requirement for a valid civil marriage is that there be a bride and groom (leaving aside civil partnerships for the moment) and two witnesses. If a small wedding party such as this goes to a restaurant for a meal after the ceremony, no more is required than a suitable and brief toast to the bride and groom, made by one of the other participants, followed perhaps by a few brief words of thanks by the bride and/or groom.

The late marriage

Obviously, not all couples marry when they are young. A bride or groom may have chosen not to get married until they are well into middle age, or they may not have found the right marriage partner until then. In many cases, a bride will have been living away from her parents' home for some years while pursuing a career, so she will hardly be 'leaving home' to embark on her married life in the same way as a bride of fifty or a hundred years ago would have done, even though her father may have 'given her away' during the marriage ceremony. And of course not all couples marry before living together: a bride and groom may have been partners for some years before deciding to get married, so the groom is already well established as part of the bride's family.

In such circumstances, while the bride's parents may well be at the wedding ceremony, it may be felt that a full-blown 'father of the bride' speech is not quite appropriate in the circumstances. No jokes, no amusing or embarrassing anecdotes, no welcoming of the groom into the family; at most, just a few words to express the bride's parents' happiness on the occasion of their daughter's wedding, and a toast to the bride and groom. Similarly, the best man (if there is one) may not feel that he needs to make a speech either, and may simply add his good wishes to those of the bride's father, and read out any messages that have been received from absent well-wishers. (If it's a small wedding group, the messages can simply be passed round the table for everyone to read.)

The second marriage

Second (or third, or fourth . . .) marriages occur because of either divorce or bereavement. Either situation calls for tact and sensitivity, and here again the full range and contents of the three traditional wedding speeches may not be wanted. As with the late marriage, the father of the bride and the best man may limit their speeches to expressions of happiness and congratulation, and hopes for the future happiness of the bride and groom. The bride's father may not make a speech at all, leaving it to the best man or some other relative or guest to propose the toast to the bride and groom.

Different circumstances

Different circumstances may require different speakers. For example, the toast to the bride and groom need not be proposed by the bride's father. If he is dead, for example, or for some reason not present, the speech could be made by whoever has given her away. If the bride's father is unable or unwilling to make a speech and it is felt that a speech is wanted as well as the toast, this responsibility could be given to a male relative (such as a favourite uncle) or to a close friend of the family (for example, the bride's godfather). The speech might even nowadays be given by the bride's mother. If the bride has grown-up children, it could be one of them.

If the couple have been living together before their marriage, they may well take responsibility for all the wedding arrangements and the cost of the wedding, and will therefore be acting as their own hosts, and the father of the bride may not be asked to contribute to the speeches at all.

In a second marriage, the son of the bride might give his mother away or the son of the groom might be his father's best man. If, however, he did not feel up to making a speech at the reception, someone else could be asked to stand in for him.

Again, the bride and groom might decide that it should be the bride and not the groom who should make the second of the traditional speeches, and that it should be she who proposes the toast to her bridesmaid. Now that many people travel abroad for work or leisure, there is an increasing number of marriages between speakers of different languages.

If the wedding is being held in the bride's country and the groom does not feel confident enough to make a speech in a foreign language (and the same might apply to his best man), it could be that the couple decide that it should be the bride who replies to her father's speech, or indeed they could choose to make a joint (and possibly bilingual) speech.

Civil partnerships have introduced several new factors into the traditional structure of wedding speeches. For a start you don't have a bride and groom, you have two people of the same sex who are making exactly the same commitment to each other as a bride and groom would do at a traditional wedding. Since there is no traditional bride/groom distinction, it is likely that both partners will want to say something. There may not be a best man/woman as such, though there will still need to be witnesses. If both fathers are present, it may well be that they will both want to speak, but on the other hand the toast to the couple may be proposed by a friend.

The key point to be taken from this section of 'different circumstances' is that there is no need to hold to tradition, nor to be worried about breaking with tradition. Notwithstanding anything that is said in this or any other book, **whatever is appropriate for a particular marriage or partnership in particular circumstances is always the right option.**

Toasts

As will be clear from what has been said above, not all wedding speeches end with or include toasts. The father of the bride toasts the bride and groom, the bridegroom toasts the bridesmaid, and that may be all.

However, if the bride speaks, she may like to toast her new parents-in-law or her husband; there may be a toast to absent friends after the best man reads out the well-wishers' messages; the bridegroom may toast his bride, or his in-laws. It is not necessary that everyone present join in these toasts: there is, for example, no reason why the groom cannot toast his bride alone, and no reason why the bride should not toast her in-laws, without the entire room having to get to their feet. But whenever such a personal toast is made, it should always be clear to the guests, from what the speaker says and does, that they are not involved and not expected to stand up and join in the toast. It would be embarrassing if half the guests stayed seated while the other half got to their feet somewhat uncertainly and were clearly unsure what to say or do.

When to propose the toast

A toast that the families and guests are to join in with need not come at the *end* of a speech, but that is definitely the best place for it. A well-constructed speech should in a way build up to the toast, and then once the toast has been proposed and drunk, everyone can settle down again and be ready to listen to the next speaker (if there is one).

There is probably an *expectation* that the toast will mark the end of the speech, and that is the format that we will be following in this book, but you should not feel obliged to follow this convention if, for some reason, you want your speech plan to be different. People may be surprised, even slightly confused, by any change from what is normally done, but if you remain on your feet after the toast, it will be obvious to everyone that you have something more to say.

Personal toasts, however, may well come in the middle of a speech. For example, if a bridegroom decided to drink a toast to his bride as part of his speech, he could do that at any suitable point in his speech. In fact, given that he is going to toast the bridesmaid at the end of his speech, he really *has* to toast the bride at some point before that. In such a case, he would drink the toast to the bride on his own, without inviting the rest of the room to join him (everyone has just toasted the bride and groom at the end of the father of the bride's speech). The same might apply if the bride wanted to toast her new husband or her parents or parents-in-law during her speech, though she *could* make the toast at the end of her speech, since she is not concluding her speech with any other toast.

Who to look at when proposing a toast

If you are proposing a personal toast to someone, and not inviting others to join you, then you should look at and speak directly to that person: i.e., if the bride is toasting her new in-laws, she should look at them.

On the other hand, if you are inviting the guests to join with you in a toast, you should look at the *guests* when proposing the toast:

Ladies and gentlemen,
Please join me in drinking to the health and happiness of John and Julie.

and then turn towards the person or people being toasted as you name them again:

John and Julie.

Speeches and toasts before the meal

We have assumed up to this point that the speeches will come after the meal. This is not always the case. For example, if the reception is more informal, with a buffet rather than a sit-down meal, the speeches may come before the food (and after the cutting of the cake). There is no particular necessity for this, nor any great advantage to it, but that is the way the arrangements are sometimes made.

The drawback is, of course, that some of the wedding party and the guests may be getting a bit peckish after the ceremony, depending on when they last ate, and may therefore not be quite so inclined to sit back (or perhaps stand, as at some buffet meals) and enjoy the speeches as they would be if they had already had something to eat. Speech-makers in such a situation would be well advised to keep their speeches fairly short and to the point.

Of course, another option would be to have the speeches *while* people are eating. Let them at least make a start on the buffet before the speeches begin, even if the buffet continues during and after the speeches. This is perhaps not to be recommended, though: eating doesn't always go well with speaking or listening.

Another situation in which speeches and toasts are sometimes made *before* the meal is when there is only a small wedding party who are enjoying food together in a restaurant after the wedding ceremony. There may be fewer speeches or, as was discussed in the 'Fewer speakers' section on page 12, there may be no speeches at all, but simply a short toast to the bride and groom. In such a case, the toast could easily be proposed while everyone is enjoying a drink before the meal, though it could be equally well left till after the meal. (Whatever you decide to do, make sure you don't disturb other people while you are doing it.)

2 Who introduces the speakers?

At many wedding receptions, no one introduces the speakers. At a suitable point after the meal, the father of the bride simply stands up, waits for the room to quieten down, and then delivers his speech and proposes the toast to the bride and groom. Perhaps he or someone else may rap on the table to attract everyone's attention before he starts, but that's all.

After the father of the bride has made his speech, proposed the toast and sat down, the bridegroom stands up, waits for the room to quieten down again and makes his speech before proposing the toast to the bridesmaid.

When he has sat down, the best man stands up . . . and so on.

With such a traditional format, there is no great need for anyone to introduce the speakers, because the guests know what to expect (or at least enough of them do).

If the speeches are not following this traditional format, however, and perhaps even if they are, it is wise to have someone delegated to introduce the speakers. There are various possibilities:

- Very often, the reception venue or caterers provide an official master/mistress of ceremonies or toastmaster/-mistress. It's part of the package. In that case, the MC will announce each speaker in turn.

- If there is no official MC, then there are various options. One is that the best man acts as MC, introducing the father of the bride, the bridegroom, etc. When it comes to his turn to speak, he simply stands up and begins his speech without any introduction (or the previous speaker can introduce him, or else he can make some joking reference to introducing himself as the next speaker).

- A member of one of the families may be asked to act as MC, introducing all the speakers. This is a useful way of involving someone who would not otherwise have a role to play in the wedding or the reception. For example, if the groom has two brothers or two close friends, and only one of them is to be a best man, then the other could be asked to be the MC.

- Yet another option is that the best man introduces the father of the bride, who, at the end of this speech, after the toast, introduces the bridegroom, who in turn at the end of this speech, after the toast, introduces the best man . . . and so on. This is not recommended. It would seem rather odd, for example, that the father of the bride should propose a toast to the bride and groom, and then himself announce that the groom will reply to it.

If there is an MC, make sure they know who is going to speak and in what order, and that they have been given all the speakers' names correctly.

Introducing the speakers

If you are acting as MC, you do not at any point make a speech *as the MC*. Your function is mainly to introduce the speakers (of which you will be one if you're the best man), not to entertain the guests yourself. However, depending on the circumstances and if the occasion is not too formal, you might tell a brief joke, and your introductions to the speakers could be humorous rather than serious. But that is all you should allow yourself. It's the speakers who are the main entertainers.

So, how do you introduce the speakers?

First of all, you have to let everyone know that the speeches are about to start. You should stand up at a suitable moment, therefore, and gain everyone's attention. If the room is quite large and there are a lot of people chatting, it might be useful if you had a gavel or other small hard object to bang on the table to attract attention, otherwise you might be on your feet for some time before anyone notices. (If you can't find anything else suitable, use an empty wine bottle – gently! – as a gavel. It works just as well.)

Give the room time to quieten down (don't try to talk over the noise of people chatting or moving their chairs into a comfortable position), introduce the father of the bride (or whoever is the first speaker), and sit down again. Something along these lines would do:

> *Ladies and gentlemen,*
> *We have all enjoyed an excellent meal, and it is now time for the speeches. So without further ado, I have great pleasure in asking Uncle Jim/Jim/Julie's father/Mr Smith/the father of the bride to propose the toast to the bride and groom.*

How you refer to the first speaker depends, of course, on how well you know him and on your relationship to him. It also depends on the formality of the occasion, and on how well you know the families and the guests. In a formal situation, something fairly brief would be enough:

> *Ladies and gentlemen,*
> *The father of the bride will now propose the toast to the bride and groom.*

Similarly, when you introduce the groom:

> *Ladies and gentlemen,*
> *The groom will now reply to the toast to the bride and groom and propose a toast to the bridesmaid.*

If you are not yourself one of the speakers, you might introduce the first speaker less formally with something like this:

> *Ladies and gentlemen,*
> *Fortunately – for me and for you – I don't have to make a speech this afternoon. My role is simply to introduce the speakers. So without further ado . . .*

You will have to decide, in discussion with the other speakers, whether 'Ladies and gentlemen' is appropriate for the occasion, or too formal. Perhaps a more informal 'Well, everyone . . .' would be better. See chapter five for more discussion on how to address the guests.

A more informal and amusing beginning could run along these lines:

> *Julie's dad has just asked me whether we should start the speeches now or let you all enjoy yourselves a bit longer.* [Pause for laughter – hopefully.] *I said we should start now while John can still stand up – that's his fourth bottle he's on now. He's probably trying to work out why there are twice as many people here as there were in the church.* [Again pause for laughter.]
> *So without further ado . . .*

Here is another possible amusing opening line:

> *Oscar Wilde once said that 'after a good dinner one can forgive anybody, even one's own relations'. As it's now time for the speeches, we're about to put that theory to the test!*

There are a number of other quotations relating to speeches and speech-making in part one of the Quick Reference section, page 115.

Pause between speeches

There will always be some noise between speeches – people talking, laughing, coughing, moving their seats to get more comfortable, and so on. As MC, you should allow time after a speech for the room to settle down again before announcing the next speaker.

Introducing the bride or bridesmaid

Although speeches by brides and bridesmaids are increasingly common, they are still not counted among the 'traditional' speeches that are

Troubleshooting: introducing a speaker in special circumstances

If one of the speakers is replacing someone who was to make a speech, or who the guests might have expected to make a speech, the MC (if there is one) or the speaker himself (if there is no MC) should make some brief comment that explains the circumstances:

As you know, Julie's father is not able to be with us today, as he is at this moment in hospital recovering from a serious operation. I'm glad to be able to say that he is recovering well and should be allowed home soon, and of course our thoughts go out to him this afternoon. Fortunately, Julie's Uncle Peter is an experienced father of the bride, having seen all three of his daughters married in recent years, and he kindly agreed to stand in for Dave today. So I have great pleasure in inviting Peter to speak to us and to propose the toast to the bride and groom. Ladies and gentlemen, the uncle of the bride, Peter.

or:

It is, of course, my brother Dave, Julie's father, who should be making this speech this afternoon, but as I am sure most of you know, he is not able to be with us today as he is at this moment in hospital recovering from a serious operation. I'm glad to be able to say that he is recovering well and should be allowed home soon, and of course our thoughts go out to him this afternoon. We know how disappointed he is not to be here.

Sad as I was that Dave would not be able to be here with us today, I was honoured when both Dave and Julie asked me to be a substitute father of the bride and speak on Dave's behalf this afternoon. I have, of course, known Julie since she was a baby, and . . .

expected at a wedding, so if the bride or bridesmaid is going to speak, it would not be inappropriate for the MC to comment on this when he introduces them:

> *As many of you will know, it is traditionally the best man who speaks on behalf of the bridesmaid at a wedding reception. However, times have changed, and nowadays women prefer to speak for themselves, and Julie and Emma, her bridesmaid, are no exceptions. We'll be hearing from Julie in a little while, but now I have great pleasure in inviting Emma to say a few words.*

At a formal reception, you would then end with:

> *Ladies and gentlemen, the bridesmaid.*

If Emma is the chief bridesmaid speaking on behalf of others as well as herself:

> *Ladies and gentlemen, the chief bridesmaid.*

To introduce the bride:

> *We have already heard from John this afternoon, but, as is the case in many marriages, his wife wants to have the last word! So I now have great pleasure in introducing Julie – not that she needs any introduction, as she is one half of the reason we are all here – and I am sure we will all be delighted to hear what she has to say.*

At a formal reception, you would then end with:

> *Ladies and gentlemen, the bride.*

Introducing other speakers

If you have to introduce any other speaker (the mother of the bride, the father of the groom, etc.), use some variation on the style of introduction for the bride and the bridesmaid.

Grace before the meal

If grace is to be said before the meal (see chapter three), the MC should introduce the person who will say it. If there is no MC, the best man or the bride's father should ask for silence and introduce the speaker. Something simple is all that is required:

Ladies and gentlemen,
Before the meal begins I would like to invite Mr Green[2]/Julie's Uncle Peter to say grace for us.

or:

Now that we are all seated, and before the meal is served, if I could ask for silence, I would like to invite Mr Green/Julie's Uncle Peter to say grace for us.

Cutting the cake

After the speeches (at a sit-down meal) or perhaps before the speeches (at a buffet), the MC announces the cutting of the cake. A brief announcement is all that is needed:

Ladies and gentlemen,
The bride and groom will now cut the cake.

[2] Please note that in British English, unlike American English, it is not correct to refer to a member of the clergy as 'Reverend Green'. It should be 'Mr Green', 'Dr Green', 'Mrs Green', etc. (See page 49 for more about correct forms of address.)

3 Saying grace

Depending on the religious beliefs (or lack of them) of the two families concerned, a grace may or may not be said before the meal. If the meal is an informal buffet, no grace is required, unless there are strong feelings in one or other family that there should be.

If grace is to be said, and a minister of religion is present (whether the person who conducted the marriage ceremony, or a member of one of the families, or a wedding guest), they should be invited to perform this duty. However, rather than simply announcing them without any warning at the start of the meal, it would be courteous to tell them earlier on that you would like them to say the grace and establish that they are happy to, although any member of the clergy is likely to be well prepared for such a request.

If there is no minister present, grace may be said by father of the bride or the father of the groom, by one of the mothers, or by a brother or sister of the bride or groom. It could be said by the best man, but if the best man is acting as MC, it is best done by someone else. How about an uncle or grandfather or godparent? (It's a good way of involving another member of one or other family.) Even a child might be asked to do it if you can be sure that they won't take stage-fright on the day – give them and their parents plenty of warning, so that they have time to choose a suitable grace and practise it.

There are examples of graces you can use or adapt in part five of the Quick Reference section, page 139.

4 Preparing your speech

It's now time to turn our attention to the speeches themselves. There are four key things you need to know about a wedding speech:

- how to write it

- what to put into it (and what not to)

- how to deliver it

- what toast (if any) to propose with it

In this chapter we will talk about how to gather material for your speech in preparation for the writing stage, which will be discussed in the next chapter. In chapter six we will discuss how to practise and deliver your speech for maximum impact. Chapters seven to eleven will cover in more detail the contents of the various speeches and in part three of the Quick Reference section we will provide a selection of toasts that go with them.

A word of warning and encouragement

Do not, under any circumstances, try to deliver an off-the-cuff speech. Always have it written and well rehearsed. But don't be afraid to alter it on the day and add in ad-libs as you go along. Something may happen on the wedding day that you will want to refer to, or something may be said in one of the preceding speeches that you will want to respond to in yours. So long as you keep to the basic structure of the speech you have written, and don't go so far off at a tangent that you lose your place altogether, appropriate ad-libs will add to the fun and enjoyment.

When to start work on the speech?

That's simple: **now!** It is never too soon to make a start on writing your speech. The sooner you start, the more relaxed you can be about it. Leaving it to the last minute is the surest way of getting into an unproductive panic. In fact, it is a very good idea to have the speech written, if possible, some weeks before the wedding and then to leave it to one side for a while. When you come back to it nearer the day, you will be able to look at it with a fresh eye, and you may spot things that you want to alter or improve.

What *not* to do

First of all, two words of warning about what you should *not* do:

- **Do not sit down at your computer, or at a table with a blank piece of paper, and expect to write your speech straight off from the beginning through to the end.** The chances are, you will still be staring at a blank screen or a blank sheet of paper an hour or two later while you try to think up that great opening line you want for your speech. Your opening line has to be the first thing you *say*, but it doesn't have to be the first thing you *write*.

- **Do not wait for inspiration.** Thomas Edison, the inventor of the lightbulb, once said that 'genius is one per cent inspiration and ninety-nine per cent perspiration'. The same is true of writing a speech. If you start work on your speech, inspiration will come; if you decide not to start work on your speech *until* inspiration comes, you could wait a long time.

   If the ideas don't come at first, don't sit despairing at your desk. Leave the speech alone, and let your subconscious mind work on it for a few days. You'll be amazed at how the very words and ideas you are looking for can unexpectedly come to mind.

How to set about it

The key to speech-writing is to split the process up into a number of smaller jobs. That way, the work stays under control and is much less daunting. So, how do you set about it?

- First of all, you will need **something to jot down your ideas in,** as and when they occur to you. Buy a small notebook that you can carry around with you. If you keep your speech constantly at the back of your mind, you will be surprised how many ideas you get. Whenever an idea for the speech occurs to you, write it down in the notebook before you forget it.

- Second, you will need **a larger notebook or a folder of paper or a computer file** to which you will transfer all your ideas from the small notebook, along with any other ideas that occur to you when you are working on your speech.

- Third, in this larger notebook, folder or file, you will need to create **a skeleton outline of your speech,** i.e. the main headings for all the elements your speech will, or might, include. These are described in detail from chapter seven onwards, but we could take some of the headings for the best man's speech as an example here:

  - opening lines
  - thanks to groom on behalf of bridesmaid
  - thanks to groom on behalf of self and ushers
  - congratulations to bride and groom
  - something complimentary about bride
  - thanks to groom for invitation to be the best man
  - anecdotes about the groom
  - interesting/amusing occurrences during the wedding preparations
  - jokes that could be used
  - quotations that could be used

It doesn't matter whether all these elements are in the order you will want them in your final speech. In fact, at this stage, you don't *know* what order you will want them to be in, or whether you will even want them all. That comes later. What you are doing at this point is setting up a structure and system which will allow you to file all your ideas efficiently under their appropriate headings, so that you can easily find them again when you want to consider them at the speech-writing stage.

- The fourth stage is to begin collecting material for your speech.

    - **Whenever you have an idea that you might use, add it to the file under the correct heading,** so that all the material for each section of your speech is gathered together in one place: that is to say, all the possible opening lines are together, all the possible jokes are together, all the possible anecdotes are together, the names of all the people you have to thank are together, and so on. Don't try to organise the material any more than that at this stage; just get everything down on paper or into your computer file.

    - **Any idea is a good idea.** This is the brainstorming part of the speech-writing process. Don't reject any story, any joke, any anecdote, any usable idea, even if you think you will probably reject it later on. For example, a really terrible and probably unusable joke might later on bring to mind a better and potentially usable one, or if it is slightly risqué you might eventually think of a way of toning it down a bit to make it suitable for the company you will be talking to. Similarly, a not very amusing anecdote might in a couple of weeks' time suggest a better one.

Obviously, as you build up your files, some sections will have more material in them than others. You will probably have more possible jokes, quotations and anecdotes than you have ideas for other parts of the speech. But that doesn't matter for the moment. Also, as ideas come to you, you may want to set up further files for categories of material you hadn't thought of at first.

People to mention

Make a list of people you have to mention or thank in your speech. In a second marriage, for example, if the couple have children, they should be mentioned in the speeches in an appropriate way – the father of the bride may be a grandfather, or now a step-grandfather; the groom may just have become a step-father – and the children, especially young children, should be reassured that they are an important part of a now larger family.

Make sure you include everyone you should mention. It would be a terrible faux pas to give a long list of thank yous and omit some key person who has contributed a lot to the success of the day. Similarly with compliments: while, for example, it is not necessary for the two mothers to be complimented on how wonderful they look in *every* speech, it would be a great pity if no one paid them a compliment in any of the speeches, while on the other hand praising the bride and the bridesmaid. Check with the other speakers who is going to mention whom.

Make sure you get everyone's name right, and in the case of uncommon or peculiar names, make sure you know how to pronounce them correctly.

Sources of inspiration and information

You have your files, and now you need to find material to file in them. Where are you going to get the ideas you need? Let's look at the speech material you might use category by category.

Anecdotes

The main source of anecdotes is surely your own memory. If you are speaking at a wedding reception, you must have known the bride or groom for some time (their whole life if you're a parent). There must be *some* incident in or aspect of their life that would make an interesting or amusing story. Who did the bride want to marry when she was a little girl? Who was the groom's favourite sports personality?

If you can't think of anything, perhaps photos in a photograph album will jog your memory: *Oh yes, there's that cottage in France where we stayed when Julie was six. And I remember now, she went off on her own one day and got lost, and we had to call the police, and . . .*

If that doesn't help, ask other members of the family or friends of the bride or groom if they can remember any interesting or amusing incidents. Someone is bound to have a tale to tell.

If you are the best man or the bridesmaid, you could talk about how you met the bride or groom, how you came to be friends, how the groom behaved differently after he had met the bride (and vice versa), the moment you knew it was serious, etc. There could be some behind-the-scenes stories about the wedding preparations or a story about something that happened during the stag party or hen night (though some of the goings-on at the stag/hen party are better not divulged).

Jokes

There are (at least) four types of joke that can be included in a wedding speech: jokes you tell, jokes at someone's expense, spoofs, and 'oops, that's not part of my speech'. We'll look at all of these.

Jokes you tell

Let's face it: some people are good at telling jokes, and some just aren't. Which are you? If you are not a natural joke-teller, it might be a mistake simply to lift a joke from a book or a website or repeat one you have heard somewhere before, as you may not tell it well enough to get a laugh. **Nothing falls flatter than a badly told joke.**

If you do write a joke or two into your speech, there are some important things to remember:

• Don't tell long jokes. You may lose your audience, or their interest, somewhere along the way.

• For the same reason, don't make the joke too complicated: some jokes that you may find in books or on websites are really better read rather than heard.

- Avoid in-jokes that only a few people will understand. (Will everyone get the joke? Will people feel left out if they don't?)

- Don't feel that a joke you use has to relate to marriage, weddings, or husbands and wives. They can relate to anything: the groom's job, the bride's hobbies, something that has been mentioned in a story you've just told . . . absolutely anything.

  There are a few marriage- and wedding-related jokes in part two of the Quick Reference section (page 127), but it is beyond the scope of this book to supply you with anything more than that very small sample. Go to a library or a bookshop and look for joke books, or go onto the Internet where you will find a huge supply of both suitable and totally unsuitable material. Search for 'wedding jokes', 'marriage jokes', or if you want to make jokes about the bride's or groom's profession or hobbies, try 'lawyer jokes', 'accountant jokes', 'nurse jokes', 'football jokes', 'fishing jokes', etc.

- Avoid jokes that involve funny accents or dialect unless you are quite sure you can carry them off amusingly. And if you do use dialect words, make sure everyone understands the joke. For example:

  '. . . she ate another slice of bara brith! (For our English guests, I should perhaps explain that "bara brith" is a sort of fruity bread that we have here in Wales.)'

- Don't include *too* many jokes in your speech. You're speaking at a wedding reception, not performing a stand-up comedy routine.

- Old jokes aren't necessarily a bad thing. You will probably get a groan rather than a laugh, but there's no harm in that. If you use a joke you know everyone will have heard before, try also to include a joke that your listeners *won't* know.

- Avoid any joke that has the slightest possibility of causing offence. Take account of your *whole* audience – their ages, their backgrounds, their probable sensitivities. For example, an 'adult' joke might make the adults laugh, but there might be parents present who would prefer their children not to have heard it (and perhaps also grown-up children present who would have preferred that their elderly parents hadn't heard it!). Some jokes are definitely better suited to the stag party or hen night than the wedding reception.

If you are making a speech at a wedding of mixed religion, race or culture, your task is that much more difficult. You must check to ensure that nothing you might say could give offence to family or guests who belong to a different culture from your own. You would be well advised to try out your speech, or at least any potentially controversial parts of it, on a member of the family to make sure.

Troubleshooting: possible taboos

It's beyond the scope of any book to lay down hard and fast rules about what is or is not a suitable joke for a wedding speech. Knowing the people who will be there, you will have to use your own judgement for that. But for an average wedding reception, with a range of guests of different ages, different backgrounds, different lifestyles, different beliefs, there are some probable no-no's, to be avoided unless you are *absolutely* sure (that's *100 per cent sure*) that a joke on such a topic will cause no offence:

- No jokes about religion, politics, illness, death, broken marriages and divorce (you're at a wedding, for heaven's sake!), extra-marital relationships and illegitimate children (same reason), mothers-in-law, and so on.

- No racism, sexism, ageism, etc.

You can add to these lists yourself – it's just a matter of tact and common sense. Find out if there are any issues within either of the families or affecting any of the guests that would make a joke on a particular topic inappropriate.

Of course there can be exceptions to any rule: a joke by the best man about the bridegroom's political affiliations might go down very well, just as well as a joke about the football team he supports, for example.

Is a mother-in-law joke never acceptable? That depends on the mothers-in-law who will be present (and that means *all* the mothers-in-law, not just the newly-weds' mothers-in-law) and how well you know them. There might be an excellent mother-in-law joke that just fits the bill and will get everyone laughing, including the mothers-in-law.

How rude or risqué or (let's call a spade a spade) downright dirty can your jokes be? Only you can decide. You know the audience. (And if you *don't* know your audience well enough, the answer is obvious – don't use the joke.)

Remember the Golden Rule of speech-writing: **if in doubt, leave it out.**

Jokes at someone's expense

The rule about this is quite simple: *don't* **make jokes at someone else's expense.** Don't even make jokes that someone might *think* was at their expense. So, for example, you don't go to the reception with this great joke about two fat ladies, because, guess what? – the bride's two great-aunts are there, and yes, they're both very large ladies. There goes the joke that you thought would be the highlight of your speech.

Of course, an exception to the general rule about not making jokes at anyone's expense is the best man's speech. The best man is usually *expected* to make fun of the bridegroom and to tell jokes at his expense. But don't let it get out of hand: a little light-hearted banter is one thing, but making the groom look a complete fool is quite another.

Spoofs

Perhaps you could introduce into your speech something that relates to the bride's or groom's employment. For example, if the bride is an estate agent, you could write a spoof of them as a 'desirable property',

Troubleshooting: more taboos

No jokes about fat people, skinny people, tall people, bald people, spotty people, Irish people, Yorkshire people . . . *unless*, of course, you are very sure of your audience. Remember that while your balding father-in-law might laugh uproariously at a joke about bald heads and combovers, there might be someone else present who is very sensitive about being bald. Always run your jokes past a member of both families to make sure. If you don't want to actually tell anyone your great joke before the day, all you need to do is ask if a joke about baldness (or whatever) would be likely to offend anyone.

based on the sort of language used in descriptions of houses for sale (which you can find in newspapers and on lawyers' and estate agents' websites):

> *This is a charming and well-proportioned property, about twenty-five years old. Of particular note is the large balcony. The property has been well looked after, but might now benefit from some upgrading and renovation. There is a play area at the front and stunning views to the rear* . . . [Part of that last sentence might not be suitable for all occasions!]

Similarly, for a teacher, write an amusing report card about them. For a doctor or a nurse, read out a 'prescription for a happy marriage' (you could base it on the Rules for a Happy Marriage on page 137); similarly for a cook, there could be a 'recipe for a happy marriage'. For a lawyer or a trade union official, you could read their 'marriage contract'. For a lawyer, a police officer, or a prison officer, you could read out their 'sentence'. And so on.

Oops, that's not part of my speech

As an example of this, the best man might address the bridegroom as follows:

> *John, I've known you a long time, and I probably know you better than almost anyone else here. What can I say about you?* [Turn over to what should be the next sheet of your notes.] *You're nothing but an ignorant, two-faced, conniving, free-loading waste of space.* [Pause to look at notes, confused.] *Oh, no, wait a minute. That's not part of my speech. That's a letter I wrote to my Member of Parliament/local councillor.* [Turn over to next sheet.] *What I meant to say was: John, you're a really great guy . . .*

It's not exactly a new and original idea, but if acted out properly, it can raise a laugh.

Quotations and one-liners

As an alternative to a joke, why not use an apt or amusing quotation or one-liner? One-liners and short quotations, being shorter than jokes, are easier to get across to an audience. A good one-liner is far better than a poor joke.

Don't use long quotations: like long jokes, they can be a bit boring, and your listeners may get lost in the middle somewhere. You can always miss out bits of a quotation, or alter it to suit your purposes: it's a wedding speech you're writing, not a work of literature, so who cares about strict accuracy? And as with jokes, it is better to avoid ones that require funny accents, unless you are sure you can do the funny accents well and that they won't offend anyone.

You will find a large selection of interesting and amusing quotations and one-liners in part one of the Quick Reference section at the end of this book. They are, for convenience, listed under various headings such as 'Love', 'Marriage', 'Advice to a husband', and so on. If you take a look through it, you will probably find the very one (or two, or three) you need for your speech. Pick out any that appeal to you and put them in the correct section of your speech file.

Even if you don't use any of these quotations or one-liners in your speech, you might find that a quotation you don't want to use reminds you of a joke or a story you *could* use. And you can always adapt the one-liners, find others, or even write your own – they don't have to be something that someone famous has said:

John has apparently promised Julie that after today he won't drink any more. Mind you, he hasn't said he'll drink any less!

Julie says she doesn't mind if John plays away from home, so long as it's only on a football pitch!

Other interesting material

Apart from the jokes, quotes and anecdotes, there is a wealth of good speech material out there if you only look around:

- Names: many names have interesting meanings (*George* means 'farmer'; *Beverley* means 'beaver meadow'), and it could be amusing to comment on the meanings associated with the bride's and groom's names. Find a book about names in your local library or a bookshop, or look in a dictionary such as *The Chambers Dictionary*.

  Or how about this for another angle on the theme of names?:

  Some people name their children after the place where they are conceived. It's lucky for John his mum and dad didn't think of doing that, or else Julie would be married to Skegness!

- Horoscopes: find out the bride's and groom's star signs and the characteristics and traits associated with them. Do they match the characters of the couple themselves, and are the couple really compatible? (Don't go too far with this in case the newly-weds take it too seriously.)

  Alternatively, you could find the bride's and groom's horoscopes on the day of the wedding and see if there is anything interesting or amusing about them; if there isn't, you can always invent something yourself:

I looked up John's horoscope this morning and it read: 'Be careful not to enter into any long-term commitments today.' Perhaps I should have mentioned that to him earlier!

- Newspapers: if you find back numbers of newspapers, you may find interesting events that happened on the days the bride and groom were born, or the day they got engaged, or the day of the wedding:

Do you know, ten years ago this very day . . .

For events even further back in time, a 'book of days' is a useful source of ideas. Some are published as books, but you can also find some on the Internet: search for 'book of days'. Here are examples of what you might find:

Did you know, ladies and gentlemen, that on this very day in 1979, snow fell in the Sahara Desert!

Today is St Boniface's Day. St Boniface is the patron saint of brewers.

Today in 1934, Donald Duck made his first appearance.

With luck, you will hit on an event that you will be able to relate in some way to the bride and groom.

- Search on the Internet for 'wedding disasters'. You could follow a story about something that happened during the wedding preparations with another story that you have found in your search (or again, you could invent a story yourself – who cares if it's not true?):

John and Julie may have had one or two problems to deal with over the past few months, but that's nothing compared to what happened to one couple I've read about. It seems that . . .

- Another source of amusement is old books on marriage etiquette and household tips, or giving advice to newly-weds. You may find these in a library or a second-hand bookshop. There are a couple of examples in part four of the Quick Reference section (page 136).

- And finally (at least for this book – for you, the possibilities are limitless if you use your imagination) there are many interesting wedding traditions and superstitions that you could find in books and on the Internet, and bring into your speech. For example, how about this traditional saying about wedding days?

> *Monday for wealth,*
> *Tuesday for health,*
> *Wednesday the best day of all.*
> *Thursday for losses,*
> *Friday for crosses,*
> *And Saturday for no luck at all.*

You would, of course, be advised to quote this saying only if the wedding day is on a Monday, Tuesday, or Wednesday! In fact, you should as a rule **only quote superstitions and traditions that bode well for the marriage,** not ones that predict disaster.

Here is an old traditional poem about the months that one marries in:

> *Marry when the year is new,*
> *Always loving, kind, and true.*
>
> *When February birds do mate,*
> *You may wed, nor dread your fate.*
>
> *If you wed when March winds blow,*
> *Joy and sorrow both you'll know.*
>
> *Marry in April when you can,*
> *Joy for maiden and for man.*
>
> *Marry in the month of May,*
> *You will surely rue the day.*
>
> *Marry when June roses blow,*
> *Over land and sea you'll go.*
>
> *They who in July do wed,*
> *Must labour always for their bread.*

Whoever wed in August be,
Many a change are sure to see.

Marry in September's shine,
Your living will be rich and fine.

If in October you do marry,
Love will come but riches tarry.

If you wed in bleak November,
Only joy will come, remember.

When December's showers fall fast,
Marry and true love will last.

(Most months are OK, but March is a bit iffy, and the prediction for May definitely rules out quoting this poem at a May wedding.)

Here are a few interesting wedding traditions and superstitions (again ignoring any that forecast doom and disaster):

It is said that whichever of the newly-weds is the first to buy some-thing after the wedding will be the dominant one in the marriage. Some brides make sure of being the first by buying a pin or some other small item from the bridesmaid right after the ceremony!

When the bride is leaving for the wedding ceremony, taking one last look in the mirror is said to ensure good luck.

Among the things that bring good luck if they are seen on the way to the wedding are rainbows, black cats and chimney sweeps.

It is lucky if the bride finds a spider in her wedding gown. (A lot of brides might disagree!)

And here are one or two more, with ways you might use them in your speech:

It's said that a cat sneezing in front of a bride on the day before her wedding is a sign of good luck. We tried that with Julie last night, but unfortunately she's allergic to cats, and it was her that sneezed over the cat! Tradition doesn't say whether that brings good luck or not, but the cat wasn't very pleased.

Some people say it's bad luck for a wedding guest to refuse a piece of the wedding cake. So all of you who are worrying about your diets, you've got a day off today. You have to eat the cake!

You all know, of course, that you should tie a horseshoe to the going-away car for good luck. I saw that done at a wedding recently, but the horse wasn't very happy – he was still wearing the shoe!

Some people say that if you take a hen into a couple's new home and make it cackle, that'll bring them good luck. So, I just want to warn John and Julie that they may get a wee surprise when they get back from their honeymoon. They may not just have their breakfast in bed, they may find something laying their breakfast in their bed!

You can, of course, invent some 'traditions' yourself for your speech, the odder the better so long as they are apt or amusing.

Variety is the spice of life (and speeches): how to make your speech stand out

Let's just mention here one or two ways you could make your speech different (and more memorable):

- If you have the talent for it, you could write your speech (or even just part of it) as poetry. Or you could turn it into song and sing it. Or sing a couple of lines or a verse or two from a popular song you know.

- We've already mentioned (page 10) that if there are two or more best men, they could make a joint speech. But even if there is only one best man, he needn't make the whole 'best man' speech on his own. He could be joined by one or two of the bridegroom's friends and they could make a joint speech.

- When describing the bride or groom, don't just use words like 'lovely', or 'beautiful, or 'handsome': use the full resources of the English language – not to show off, but just for fun. For this you will need a large thesaurus, such as *Roget's Thesaurus*. (Try your library, or a bookshop.) For example, instead of saying the bride looks 'lovely', you could say that she is '**pulchritudinous**' (pronounced 'pul-kri-*tyood*-in-us'; it means 'beautiful') or a '**vision of pulchritude**', or that she is '**callipygian**' or '**callipygous**' (pronounced 'ka-li-*pij*-an' and 'ka-li-*pie*-gus'; they both mean she's got a lovely bottom). Use a whole string of descriptive words and phrases: say she's 'a smasher, a stunner, a scorcher, a looker, a dreamboat, a cutie, a honey, a peach, sex on a stick, an über-babe'. Lay it on thick, and use the thesaurus for suitable words and phrases to use.

- You could use some props:

  - Taking out a clock or an egg-timer at the start of your speech might raise a laugh. You could bring out a kitchen timer, set to go off halfway through your speech, and put it down in front of you. When it rings, you could say something like:

    That's just to waken up anyone who's fallen asleep from boredom, or drink.

    or:

    That's just to let you all know that we're halfway through my speech now, in case you were getting anxious.

  - You could bring out a roll of toilet paper:

    This is the first version of my speech. So you can see where I did most of my thinking!

  - You could use a pile of paper to joke about the length of your speech – or its shortness:

    [Pick up a pile of paper from the floor, and plonk it on the table.] *This was going to be my speech today, but I let John read it over and he took out all the stories that he didn't want Julie to hear.* [Lift off half the pile, and put it aside.] *Then I let Julie's dad read over what was left, and he took out all the jokes that he didn't think Julie's mum should hear.* [Put aside another part of the pile of paper.] *So* [lift up the few sheets of paper that actually are your speech notes], *I'm afraid this is all I'm left with.*

- Instead of, or as well as, props, you could use other visual aids. For example, the father of the bride's speech could be accompanied by slides or a video showing episodes from his daughter's life: the naked baby on the rug, the toddler in nappies, the first day at school, the seven-year-old beach babe in the bikini, that picture of her on the donkey on the beach at Redcar, the first party dress, the first adult party dress, the sixteen-year-old beach babe in the bikini . . . and so on.

There are, of course, some possible problems to be aware of. Slides and videos need electrical equipment, and electrical equipment can break down (remember Murphy's Law: if anything can go wrong, it will). So you need a Plan B in case the visuals don't work on the day, i.e. a speech that doesn't *totally* rely on them. And you will need to check on the layout of the room beforehand: will all the guests be able to see the screen? Where can you set up the projector? And can you make the room dark enough for the pictures to be seen clearly? (And if the room *is* darkened, how are you going to read your notes? Take a torch.)

5 Writing your speech

You've been gathering your thoughts for some days, weeks, or even months now, and your files are (hopefully) full of useful, usable material. Now it is time to write your speech. So, take a new sheet of paper or open a new file on your computer, and prepare to write. But **don't imagine that what you are going to write now is the finished speech**: it may take several drafts (at least two or three) before you have created a speech you are satisfied with.

First things first

Before you make a start to your first draft, there are some things you have to find out or decide for yourself:

- Firstly, what should the *tone* of the speech be? Should it be slightly formal or quite informal? What tone and style are the other speakers going to adopt? It would be wise if all the speakers adopted the same tone: it would be odd if the bride's father delivered a rather formal speech and the bridegroom replied in a very informal and jokey style (though there is no need to match each other exactly, and the best man can perhaps allow himself some leeway to be more informal than the others).

  But remember – you've still got to be yourself, so don't try to be something you aren't. If you are the bride's father, you are the bride's father, not one of the gang. Don't try to be.

- Think about the setting for the meal, and whether that will affect what you say and how you say it. If the meal is being held in a public restaurant where other people are eating, for example, the bride and groom may not want embarrassing anecdotes about them broadcast to a roomful of strangers. And of course, where other diners may be able to hear what is said, the speech should not include anything risqué: you don't want to cause offence.

- How many speeches are there going to be? The more speeches, the shorter any one of them should probably be. Either you include fewer elements in your speech, or you say less about each one.

- It is often recommended that the speakers all confer with one another before writing their speeches so that they don't end up telling the same jokes or recounting the same anecdotes. This is a wise precaution, as in a sense the after-dinner speakers are putting on a show together, and no one wants to listen to two or three speakers all tell the same story about how the couple met when John literally fell at Julie's feet at the bus stop that icy morning three years ago. But you don't need to take this to the point of reading over each other's speeches. It's enough if you just mention to one another what jokes and stories you intend to tell (and the best man should certainly keep a few extra stories about the bridegroom up his sleeve and spring them on him unexpectedly at the reception).

Some speech dos and don'ts

- Don't try to impress people or to seem cleverer than you are, or you may come across as pompous or patronising. Just be yourself. Use everyday language, as you would when you're talking to friends and family (because that is what you *are* doing at the reception).

- If you do poke fun at someone (as the best man might do to the groom), you should perhaps mention some of their good points and successes as well.

- Don't swear or blaspheme.

- Don't lecture your listeners, or use the speech as a platform for your own opinions. It's neither the time nor place.

- Don't tell lies. Embroidering the truth a little is OK, though, as are remarks that are clearly meant to be taken as jokes rather than facts. This one might go down well if there is a rugby connection at the wedding (but it might *not* be suitable, depending on who else is there):

I don't know if you all know that Julie's bridesmaid Emma used to play for a women's rugby team. She was a hooker.

Tact and sensitivity (and a bit of common sense)

It should go without saying – but let's say it anyway – that all wedding speeches should be written with tact and sensitivity. Never forget – and this applies especially to the best man or bridesmaid or any other friend of the couple who may be making a speech – that you may be privy to some information about them that others are not aware of and that the bride or groom would not *want* them to be aware of. **You are in a privileged position – don't abuse it.**

The things *not* to mention in a speech are impossible to list in full. This is where you have to use not just tact and sensitivity, but plain common sense as well. But for example:

- Do not mention any serious failings or failures on the part of the bride or groom.

- Do not mention anything the least bit dubious about their past. If it is already known to others, fine; if it is not known, the reception is not the time to make it known.

- Do not mention past partners and relationships, except perhaps in a very general and facetious way. For example, it would probably be considered bad taste for the best man to mention the groom's relationship with a particular past partner or girlfriend, but it would do no harm for him to make a joke about the groom's 'previous girl-friends' in a very unspecific way.

• If the couple have been living together before the marriage, do not assume that this is common knowledge in both families. While an unmarried couple living together is less of an issue than it was thirty or forty years ago, there may still be relatives of the bride or the groom who would be upset by such behaviour and who have therefore not been told. So before making any remarks in your speech about what the bride and groom have been doing before their marriage, check that this will not be news to anyone present at the wedding.

• In the case of a second or subsequent marriage, the whole tone of any remarks that are made in a speech should possibly be rather less facetious than in other circumstances, given that the happiness of the occasion may nevertheless be accompanied by a tinge of sadness over a past relationship that has failed or a much-loved previous husband or wife who has died. This is not to say that the speech should be over-formal or solemn; there is no need for that. But while writing your speech, always keep in mind where the couple are coming from. It's a happy day for them, but . . .

• If not the bride or groom, there might be someone else present who has suffered a bereavement – one or other of the bride's or groom's parents, for example, may have died. Or they may be divorced. A wedding can be a difficult time for such a person, no matter how happy they are for their child. Be sensitive about this.

How to start your speech

Addressing your audience

When you stand up to speak, the very first thing you have to say is some form of greeting to your audience – the two families and the guests. How you do this depends on how formal your speech is meant to be.

At a very formal wedding and wedding reception, you should begin your speech with 'Ladies and gentlemen'. If there are important guests who should be mentioned by name, name them before the 'Ladies and gentlemen':

Your Grace, Monsignor McNeill, Father Porter, Ladies and gentlemen, . . .

Troubleshooting: correct forms of address

If you have to specifically address a distinguished guest at the beginning of your speech, it is important that you do so correctly. Check the correct forms of address in a book such as *Debrett's Correct Form*. Ask your local librarian.

More informally, you could begin your speech with something like 'Dear friends', 'Dear friends and family', or simply 'Well, good evening, everyone'.

The groom might want to address his parents and his wife's parents and close family by name (as might the best man if he is a member of the family and not just a friend of the groom):

Mum, Dad, Peter, Moira, Jonathon, and all of you who are here celebrating with us this evening . . .

You could make a very informal and jokey introduction:

I was going to start my speech with the conventional 'ladies and gentlemen', but it seemed unfair to cut so many of you out/but I wanted to address my speech to all of you.

When I came to write my speech, I wasn't sure how to start. I know the usual opening is 'ladies and gentlemen', but that sounded much too formal for a gathering like this, and in any case I know some of you far too well to address you as 'ladies' or 'gentlemen'. You know who you are!

Ladies and gentlemen (that's everyone at the top table), friends and family (that's you out there), and scrubbers and chavs (that's that lot over there in the corner) . . .

Dear friends and family, and the couple at the back that I've never seen before and are either gatecrashing or at the wrong wedding . . .

This one works for football enthusiasts (you choose which football team to name):

Dear friends, family, lovers of football, and supporters of Broadside United . . .

A further option is simply to launch straight into your speech without any opening address at all. Just stand up and hit them with a punchy opening line, such as the Oscar Wilde quote we've seen in chapter two (if the MC isn't using it, why not you?):

Oscar Wilde once said that 'after a good dinner one can forgive anybody, even one's own relations'. I'm just about to put that theory to the test!

This brings us to the next part of your speech, which is . . . the opening line.

The opening line

Try to think of an opening line that will get people's attention and make them laugh. (Not 'Unaccustomed as I am to public speaking . . .', unless, for example, everyone knows you *are* accustomed to public speaking, in which case that line might just scrape a laugh, or a groan.) So, here are a few possible starters:

Ladies and gentlemen,
    (Well, how do you like the speech so far?)

Dear friends and family,
    (Does that mean that family aren't friends?)

You've heard two excellent speakers so far this evening, but now I'm afraid you've got me.

I've really sweated and suffered over this speech, and now it's your turn.

Ladies and gentlemen,
   I know that's maybe a bit too formal for this occasion, but I'm hoping that if I flatter you at the beginning of my speech, you'll forgive me for the rest of it!

Well, everyone, this is the moment Mary and I have both been dreading. My speech. I've been dreading making it, and she's been dreading having to listen to me. So I'll be brief. [At this point, you could place a large egg-timer and/or a clock on the table in front of you. See page 43 for further discussion about props you could use with your speech.]

The examples above can be used in any speech, but here are some ideas specifically for the groom and the best man.

For the groom:

My mother told me this morning that this should be the happiest day of my life. I asked Dad if that meant it was all downhill from here.

I'm not going to say much, because if I talk for too long I may develop a serious breathing problem – Julie said she'd throttle me if I went on for more than a couple of minutes!

For the best man:

When I asked John how long my speech should be, I got a real shock. I thought he said 'forty-five minutes'! Actually, what he said was 'four to five minutes'.

There are many definitions of marriage, and some of them can give you a good opener (though you could equally well use them later on in your speech):

Marriage is said to be a union between a man and woman. If it is, I know which one of us is going to be the shop steward!

Marriage is like a three-ring circus. First there's the engagement ring. Then the wedding ring. And then the suffering! No, but seriously . . .

They say getting married is like trying to win the lottery. Well, if it is, I've certainly won the jackpot!

Here are some more you can put your own endings to:

They say that marriage involves a lot of give and take . . .

Marriage is for better or for worse . . .

Marriage is for richer, for poorer . . .

Of course, you needn't start your speech with a joke. You could begin with a more serious comment:

They say that marriage is a gift from heaven, and when I look at Julie and John, I can readily believe it. They are clearly in their own little bit of heaven right now.

Marriage, they say, is like gardening. You cultivate the beautiful flowers and you pull out all the weeds.

It has been said that marriage is not about finding the right partner but being the right partner.

Go for the unexpected

It can be very effective to lead your listeners to expect one thing and then deliver something quite different. One excellent speech by a father of the bride began with what seemed to be an old chestnut: *There was an Englishman, an Irishman, and a Scotsman.* This, of course, was received with good-natured groans all round. But the speech then developed in an unexpected direction with a brief family history – the father of the bride was the Englishman, his wife's father was the Irishman, and his new son-in-law was the Scotsman. The speaker wrong-footed his listeners, and so made the story that much more memorable.

The middle section

The middle section of your speech will consist of welcomes, thanks, compliments, stories, words of advice (serious or otherwise), jokes and one-liners, etc. (as outlined in chapter one), in whatever order you choose. We'll look at this section of the speech in more detail in the following chapters, but here are some general points to consider.

Welcomes

There is nothing very difficult about welcoming the guests:

> First of all, I'd like to welcome you all here this afternoon, and to thank you for sharing this exciting day with us. It's good to see so many of our friends and family here – I don't think there has been any gathering like this since we celebrated Julie's first birthday 24 years ago. And I would like to say a special welcome to Tom and Joyce, John's mum and dad, and to all their family and friends who are here celebrating with us today. I am looking forward to getting to know you all better this evening.

At this point, mention can be made of anyone who has not been able to attend the wedding:

> Of course there are some people who are not with us today, and who are greatly missed. John's cousin Trevor was recently involved in a serious car accident, and although I am pleased to say that he is well on the way to recovery, his doctors felt, much to Trev's disappointment, that it would be unwise for him to try to attend the wedding today.
>
> And I know that much in our family's thoughts this afternoon was Julie's grandmother, who sadly passed away three months ago. We all know how fond she had become of John in the time she had known him, and how much she was looking forward to seeing Julie and John married, but it was not to be. But we can be sure that she was with us in spirit this afternoon. She certainly won't have missed Julie and John's wedding, you can be sure of that!

Quotations and one-liners

If you use a quotation or one-liner, try to relate it to the bride and/or groom (or the bridesmaid, or the best man, etc.) so that it has a clear purpose; for example, the best man could say about the bridegroom:

> *As Jane Austen famously said: 'It is a truth universally acknowledged, that a single man in possession of a good fortune, must be in want of a wife.' Well, considering how rarely John buys anyone a drink down the pub, he must have a real fortune by now, so Julie has chosen well.*

> *Groucho Marx once said that 'Marriage is a wonderful institution, but who wants to live in an institution?' Well, people have often said that John should be put in an institution. Perhaps we've found the right one for him at last.*

> *Someone once said that 'No woman should marry a teetotaller'. Well, with John, Julie can certainly relax on that score.*

In general, don't use any quotation or one-liner that implies that marriages are inevitably difficult or unhappy. However, it would be quite in order for, say, a happily married father of the bride or best man to use such a quotation in order to *deny* it:

> *Someone once said that 'Marriage is like life – it's a field of battle, not a bed of roses'. Well, that certainly hasn't been my experience, and if Julie and John are as well suited to each other as Mary and I are – and I really do believe they are – their marriage will be no field of battle, even if it isn't a bed of roses every day. You do have to expect the occasional skirmish, as I am sure all the married couples here would agree.*

For this reason, a few negative quotations and one-liners have been included in part one of the Quick Reference section (page 115). Use them to deny them.

Naming names

Some of the people quoted are well-known names, others are not at all well known but are included in this book because the quotation seemed apt or amusing. For well-known names, you could say in your speech, for example:

As Robert Burns wrote in one of his poems . . .

or:

That reminds me of something Woody Allen once said . . .

For people your listeners are unlikely ever to have heard of, you might be better to say something like:

As someone once said . . .

or:

As an American writer once put it . . .

Alternatively, simply use the quotation in your speech as if it was your own thought. There is no necessity to admit that it comes from someone else unless it is a very well-known saying. And don't be afraid to cut out words you don't want or to reword the quotation slightly if you would prefer another way of saying it – it's your speech, and who's going to check up? For example, you might want to use this quotation about marriage exactly as it stands:

In every marriage more than a week old, there are grounds for divorce. The trick is to find, and continue to find, grounds for marriage.

But you might prefer a shorter version that encapsulates the thought but is less wordy:

In every marriage, there are grounds for divorce. The trick is to continue to find grounds for marriage.

Jokes

As part of the speech-writing process, try out some jokes on a few people before deciding whether or not to include them. See which ones go down best. If the jokes don't seem funny, perhaps you are not telling them the right way. Ask for help from someone whose jokes always get a laugh.

How do you introduce a joke into your speech? Ideally it should follow on smoothly from something you have just been talking about:

> *Thinking about Julie as a little girl puts me in mind of a joke I once heard. There was a little girl who once asked her grandmother: 'How old are you, Granny?' 'I'm not sure,' said her grandmother. 'I'm so old, I've forgotten how old I am.' 'Well, you'd find out if you looked in your knickers, Granny,' said the little girl. 'The label on mine says I'm five to six years old.'*

The joke is not about Julie, but it follows on easily and logically from something that has just been said about Julie.

If you have a joke you want to tell that you can't integrate easily into your speech, you can simply announce to your listeners that you are now going to tell a joke:

> *I know that every father-of-the-bride speech should have at least one anecdote about the bride, one joke, and one piece of advice. So here's my joke.*

> *Now, I know you are all expecting me to tell a joke at some point in my speech. So, just so that you aren't disappointed, here comes my joke now. Of course, the benefit of me telling you that, is that you'll know you're supposed to laugh when I get to the end of it!*

> *I'm not very good at telling jokes, but here's one I heard recently. Don't stop me if you've already heard it, because it's the only one I've rehearsed. In fact, it's the only one I can remember!*

If you don't want to tell a joke at all, you could try an excuse like this:

> *I was going to tell a joke at this point, but I hunted through dozens of joke books and I couldn't find a single joke that I could possibly tell in front of my mother/wife/mother-in-law. So passing quickly on . . .*

Anecdotes

As with jokes, there are various ways of introducing an anecdote. Here are two, one for the best man, and one for the father of the bride:

Now I know it's expected that the best man will embarrass the groom with an anecdote or two about the his past, and I wouldn't want to let you all down in that respect. And boy, have I got some good ones! I don't know if even Julie has heard some these stories before. . . .

One of the pleasures of the father of the bride's speech is that a father gets to tell some amusing stories about his daughter. Now I'm not going to embarrass Julie – much – this afternoon, but I was looking through our old photograph albums the other day and I came across a picture of Julie on a donkey on the beach at Redcar. She was about eight at the time, I think. I don't know if she remembers what happened that day, but . . .

Words of advice

In the next section, we will look at how giving some advice to the bride-groom or to the bride and groom can make a good ending to a speech, but you could also include advice, serious or humorous, in the middle of your speech. We have shown one possible introduction on page 56 under 'Jokes', but it could be used just as well to introduce an anecdote or a piece of advice (not for all three in the one speech):

I know that every father-of-the-bride speech should have at least one anecdote about the bride, one joke, and one piece of advice. So here's my piece of advice to Julie and John . . .

Or again:

Now I'm sure every married couple here would have at least one piece of good advice that they would like to give to Julie and John as they set out on their new life together. Well, here is something I recently found in a book I was reading, and I think these wise words express exactly what I want to say to them today.

The grand finale

Two of the speeches, the father of the bride's and the bridegroom's, end with a toast (see page 6). Other speeches may do. But whether or not there is a toast, it is good if you can end your speech, just as you began it, on a high note. A final amusing quotation or joke is a good way to conclude. For example, the father of the bride might turn to the bridegroom as he finishes his speech, and say:

> *And finally, a word of advice to John. Or in fact two words of advice. Remember that several excuses are always less convincing than one. And a little inaccuracy sometimes saves a great deal of explanation!* [Pause for laughter – hopefully.]
>
> *And now I would like to ask you all to join with me in a toast to the bride and groom . . .*

Alternatively, you can say something that leads straight into your toast. For example, the bridegroom, about to toast the bridesmaid, might lead into it with a compliment or two (or three . . .):

> *I'm coming to the end of my speech now, but of course, as you know, it's always the bridegroom's duty at a wedding reception to propose a toast to the bridesmaid. And a very pleasant duty it is, too. I know that Emma has been a great help and support to Julie over the past few months, and she has certainly shown the truth of the saying that 'a happy bridesmaid makes for a happy bride'. But Emma is not only cheerful and helpful, she's beautiful too, and if you look at the third finger of her left hand, you will see that it won't be long before she too walks down the aisle, with Julie as her matron of honour.*
>
> *So I'd like you all to join me now in a toast, not only to Emma, but also to her fiancé James. May they know great happiness in the years ahead.*
>
> *Emma and James.*

Go for the unexpected

Wrong-footing your listeners at the end of your speech, just as you might do at the start, is a good way of making it memorable. Imagine some people's reaction if the father of the bride ended his speech by turning to the bride and groom and saying solemnly:

> *And now I just want to give John and Julie a word of advice about what to do in bed.* [Pause for the shock ripples.] *Always remember:* [pause again] *one good turn gets most of the duvet!* [And then on to the toast.]

The first draft

In the first draft of your speech, you will begin to put your material into some sort of order, though not necessarily the order it will be in in the final version.

From your file of notes and ideas, you have to decide what material to use and what to discard (it won't necessarily be a final decision, so keep anything you think you won't use, just in case you change your mind later on).

Unlike at the material-collecting stage, it is probably a good idea at the drafting/writing stage for you to start at the beginning of the speech and try to build it up piece by piece. In that way, you will see how you can move on from one topic to the next. So, at any given point in your draft, you will be looking at what you have just written and then looking at what is left to be said and asking yourself, 'What would be the best subject to come next?'

When you were at school (if you can remember that far back), you were probably told in the English class to 'start a new paragraph when you start a new subject'. The very same applies to speech-writing. If you think of your speech as a series of subjects or themes, each of which needs one paragraph of a few sentences, the task won't seem nearly so daunting. So, when you are writing your first draft, think in paragraphs – just jot down a few sentences (or even just words and phrases) on each theme (a few compliments, the outline of an anecdote or a joke). Don't worry at this stage about exactly how you are going to link the paragraphs, but try to order them so that you can see how each subject will follow on easily and logically from what has gone before (compliment → anecdote → joke, and so on). You can also jot down comments and notes to yourself to think about at the second draft.

The first draft of the beginning of a father-of-the-bride speech might look something like this:

> *Ladies and gentlemen (Too formal? How about Dear Friends? What about family then? Mention anyone by name?)*
>
> *Start with quotation? 'Someone once said that an after-dinner speaker is a man who rises to the occasion and then stands too long' How to follow on? Something like . . . Well, I certainly hope speech rises to the occasion, but promise won't speak for long.*
>
> *First of all, say what pleasure to see guests gathered there. Particular mention John's family. Also Ruth and Bob, because come a long way?*
>
> *What to say next? Need to get round to Julie.*
>
> *Proud of Julie. Her achievements. (Which to mention? Dancing, music, college, good job. More than that – what she is – kind, considerate, puts other people first. Story about this? That time she was a Brownie? How about her love of animals? All those pets! The hippo story? The donkey?*
>
> *Animal joke to follow that? Look on Internet.*
>
> *Need to say something about John. (Julie's new pet? Maybe better not. Might be offended.) Welcome J into the family. Anecdote – how love of animals brought them together.*

And so on. Without putting any pressure on yourself, you are beginning to create a speech. It's only a skeleton, but it's taking shape. There are still decisions to be made, but you don't have to make them quite yet.

The second draft

It is when you come to the *second* draft that you fill out the details of the compliments, stories, jokes, etc. and begin to link the paragraphs so that your speech progresses smoothly from beginning to end. (You will find various ways of doing this in the examples in this book, especially in the sample speeches in chapters seven to eleven.)

Of course, you may want to change the order of subjects when you come to write a second draft, and you will polish up the way you have expressed some things, but you can't make a *better* version of your speech until you have something to make a better version of.

The beginning of your second draft might look like this:

> *Ladies and gentlemen, or perhaps I should simply say, My dear friends and family.*
>
> *Someone once said that an after-dinner speaker is a man who rises to the occasion and then stands too long! Well, I certainly hope that my speech rises to the occasion this afternoon, but I promise you I won't speak for long.*
>
> *First of all, I would like to say on behalf of Mary and myself what a great pleasure it is to see you all here today.*

And so on. You are still keeping to the paragraphs of your first draft, but now the skeleton has been fleshed out into something more like a completed speech.

After you have written out the second draft, time yourself reading it out loud at the speed at which you will speak at the reception (which should be **slightly slower than normal speaking speed**). Is it about long enough? Is it too long, or too short? If it is too long, look for something to take out or cut down; if it is too short, go back to your files and look for something to add in.

Be critical

Next, look at your speech critically and see if there is any way of improving it. (There almost certainly will be.) Do you need to rewrite parts of it? Do you need to change the order of topics? Have you chosen a good joke, or would another one in your file or joke book fit in better?

Repetitions and overused words

Check over your speech to see whether you may have overused some word or phrase. A well-known sportswoman, having won the title of sports personality of the year, once made a speech along these lines:

> *This is amazing. Thank you to all the voters. It is amazing to be here with all these fantastic sports people. I'm in awe of everyone and to win this prize is absolutely amazing.*

Given that there was a possibility she might win (even if she thought she wouldn't), she really should have done a little more work on her acceptance speech. Three *amazing*s in four short sentences was two too many. 'Nice' is another word that is often overused. (You may have been told that at school.)

If you find you have done the same sort of thing, rewrite some of it using different words. If necessary, use a good thesaurus to find suitable alternatives.

Troubleshooting: the last-minute speaker

Finally, a word to the last-minute stand-in speaker. If you have been asked to speak at fairly short notice, perhaps because one of the expected speakers has suddenly been taken ill, you should be realistic about what you can achieve in the time you have left. You can't expect to do in four days, or two days, or one day, what you could have achieved in four weeks. You will have less time to research and write your speech, and almost no time to practise it. So keep it short and keep it simple. Check in the appropriate chapter in this book what the bare minimum is that you have to say and what you must include in your speech, and concentrate on that. If you know or can find a suitable joke or quote, or can think of an amusing anecdote, well and good; if not, there is no harm done. Just do the basics. Everyone will understand.

Note to other speakers

If someone has to stand in at the very last minute, with perhaps as little as a few hours' notice, or even less, they are going to need your help. They won't have time to read this book, but you will have read it. Make sure they know what they are supposed to say in their speech – under the circumstances, the bare minimum will do, though if you can help them out with a joke, quote, or anecdote, so much the better. And when this stand-in speaker is announced, it should be mentioned that they have been asked to fill in at the last minute (for whatever reason).

The toasts and how to introduce them

The father of the bride's and the bridegroom's speeches both end with a toast, and others may do.

There are various ways of inviting your listeners to take part in a toast. When you have come to the end of your speech, whether with the killer grand finale or the complimentary lead-in (see page 58 for an example of both of these), you can simply say something along the lines of:

And now I'd like to invite you all to join me in a toast to . . .

Some people use the phrase 'Please rise and join me . . .' but this isn't really necessary as most people know that they should stand to drink a toast. Other people recommend the rather old-fashioned 'please charge your glasses (which means 'fill your glasses') and join me . . .', but it's rather a pointless phrase, since (i) many people may not know what 'charge your glasses' actually means, and (ii) by the time you have got to that point, no one has time to pick up a wine bottle and fill their glass anyway. (Glasses should be filled before or during speeches, not at the end of them when the toast is actually being proposed. You could even make a joke about this, by breaking off halfway through your speech and reminding people to check that they have something in their glass, 'because in about two minutes from now I'll be asking you to join me in a toast'.)

The toast you propose can be very simple and straightforward:

[Addressing the audience] *And now I'd like to ask you all to join me in wishing Julie and John a long and happy marriage.*
[Turn to the newly-weds] *Julie and John.*

However, you may feel that you want to propose a little more original and memorable toast:

[Addressing the audience] *And now I'd like to ask you all to join me in a toast to the bride and groom.*
[Turn to the newly-weds] *Julie and John. May the roof above you never fall in, and may you never fall out!*

You will find a selection of suitable toasts in part three of the Quick Reference section (page 131). And of course there are specialist books on toasts with a wider selection than can be included in this book, and many Internet sources as well.

6 Rehearsing and delivering your speech

Now you have written your speech, you are still only halfway to success, no matter how good the speech is on paper.

**A perfect speech must not only be well written,
it must also be well delivered.**

Your next step is to practise speaking in public (though you needn't actually have an audience at this stage if you don't want one – a mirror will do, or a video camera).

But in order to practise, you first have to know what you should do on the day: how you should stand, how you should speak, and so on. Otherwise, in practising, you might simply be getting into the way of doing everything wrong, which would be no help at all. So, in this chapter, we will first talk about how you should deliver your speech; then we will talk about how you should practise in order to get it right on the day; and finally we will consider some dos and don'ts for the day itself.

Notes to use on the day

First of all, though, you must decide what you will want to hold in your hand when you make your speech. You could, for example, have the whole thing written out, or, on the other hand, you could make do with a set of prompt cards, with only the headings and main points on them to remind you of what you want to say. There are advantages and disadvantages to both of these.

If you have the whole speech written out, you will always have a note of what you want to say next. On the other hand, though, you may be tempted to read word by word from your notes, which might make it rather flat and boring, and there will also be a tendency for you to stand with your head down and mumble into your notes instead of looking at your audience, and if you do that, no one is going to hear that brilliant one-liner you found at the back of this book, are they?

If you only use prompt cards, you will probably speak in a more natural and lively tone, but there is always the possibility of you forgetting what you intended to say under a particular heading or key point, and your speech may become rather hesitant, with long pauses while you gather your thoughts for what you want to say next.

One solution is to have speech notes that combine both styles. Have the whole speech written out as a safety precaution, so that you have everything you intend to say written down and in your hand, but have the headings and key points (such as the punchlines of jokes) written in a different colour or in larger letters. (A computer is handy for this job, as you can use letters of different sizes, types, and colours, but coloured pens and pencils will do the job just as well.) If you do write it out by hand, make sure you can read your own handwriting! Leaving a space between each line of writing is another good idea, as it will make your notes easier to read.

Whether you write out your speech in full or only have notes and headings in front of you, it is best to use large file cards rather than paper, as paper may flop or bend, but cards won't. Number the cards, so that if you drop them, you can quickly get them into the correct order again. And in case they get lost, photocopy them and put the photocopies in a safe place.

How to deliver your speech

The following are some key points to remember, which you will need to practise beforehand:

- Don't stand too rigidly when you are speaking, but don't slouch or shuffle about, either. Keep relaxed and shift your weight from one foot to the other from time to time.

- Try to look confident (even if you really feel like hiding under the table) and happy to be there. It is more likely that your audience will enjoy listening to you if you look and sound as if you are enjoying speaking to them. Smile, at least occasionally. Put on an act – and you may even fool yourself!

- Speak to your audience, don't talk into your notes. Depending on how well you know your speech after practising it and how confident you feel on the day, you may not have to look at your notes very often. But even if you are following your notes pretty carefully, you must look up and look around at your audience as well. Make eye contact with your listeners (but don't stare at any one person or you will make them feel uncomfortable).

- Speak clearly and a little louder and slower than normal. (Remember that if you are nervous on the day, you will tend to speak faster than normal, so you must practise speaking more slowly to overcome this.) Pause occasionally at appropriate points – don't gallop from one paragraph to the next. Keep the tone conversational, as though you are talking to friends – which you will be.

- Remember to breathe naturally. That may sound obvious, but if you are nervous, you may tense up without realising it and not breathe properly, which will make your speech sound as tense as you are. (Here again, practice will help you avoid this tendency.)

- Do not speak in a boring monotone. If you have followed the advice in chapters four and five, you will have written a speech in which there is a good mixture of serious and amusing material, so when speaking try to vary your tone to reflect this. You can also use hand gestures to emphasise points you make, but remember that this is just a wedding speech – you are not an orator trying to whip up a crowd.

- You will be holding your notes in one hand, but if you have the other hand free, keep it under control. If you put your hand in your pocket, don't jangle your loose change or keys. If you keep your free hand out of your pocket, don't scratch yourself, rub your nose, fiddle with your ears/hair/moustache/beard, twiddle your tie, or do anything else that would distract or annoy your listeners.

Do speakers always stand up to give their speeches?

Speakers *normally* stand up. It makes them easier to see and hear, and it is in fact much easier to give a speech standing up than it is if you are sitting down. An exceptional case would be if one of the speakers was incapacitated and unable to stand, in which case they would remain seated, and the other speakers might therefore choose to do so as well. (This needs to be discussed and decided beforehand.)

Speakers usually stand where they have been sitting, so long as everyone in the room can both see and hear them. If a speaker cannot be seen by some of the guests, then either the speaker should move to a more suitable position or those guests should be invited to move their chairs before the speeches start. (This needs to be planned in advance.)

At a buffet where there may be no top table and many of the guests may be standing or moving around, it is more necessary for the speakers to choose or be given a suitable place for speaking. They may want to be beside a table so that they have somewhere to place the glass of wine that they will need when they propose the toast.

Rehearsing your speech

Once you have written the final version of your speech and have thoroughly acquainted yourself with the guidelines on how it should be spoken, you should begin to practise it.

Make the practice conditions as close as possible to the actual conditions at the reception. For example, you will presumably be standing up to speak, so stand when you practise. You will probably be standing at a table when you speak, with your chair behind you, so if possible put a table in front of you and a chair behind you when you are practising. Decide how you are going to stand, and what you will do with your hands. If you think you might have to hold a microphone when you are speaking (and if possible you should have found that out by now), practise with something similar in one hand (you will have your notes in your other hand), holding your substitute microphone about four inches away from your mouth.

When rehearsing, watch yourself in a mirror or video yourself, so that you can see what you will look like to your audience. Many comedians and other performers do this. Remember to look at yourself in the mirror or look at the camera, and not just at your notes, because you are going to have to look at the wedding guests while you are speaking at the reception.

As well as looking at yourself, listen to yourself: are you talking very monotonously, or is there enough life and interest in your voice? (Is there, for that matter, enough life and interest in your expression when you are speaking? The two are closely related.) If you have the equipment to do it, it is a good idea to record yourself, so that you can concentrate on what you sound like.

If you are new to public speaking, don't expect to produce a brilliant performance at the first attempt, and don't become disheartened. Keep on practising until you are completely happy with your performance and are confident that you will be able to carry it off on the day. Indeed, keep on practising and you *will* be able to carry it off on the day. Remember:

Practice makes perfect.

After you have rehearsed your speech a few times on your own, you could ask a friend or relative to watch you as you practise and comment on anything they notice about your performance from a listener's point of view. You may feel nervous or awkward about doing this, but as well as drawing your attention to aspects of your delivery you may not have noticed, it may also help you overcome any nervousness you still have about speaking in front of an audience.

Once you have practised your speech a few times, you will probably know it more or less off by heart, and will only have to glance at your notes from time to time. But **don't deliberately try to memorise it**, as unless you are an experienced performer, repeating something from memory can make for a rather flat and uninteresting presentation. You don't need to know your speech off by heart; you will have your notes with you to keep you right.

While you will no doubt need to rehearse your speech several times before you are satisfied with your performance, **be careful not to over-rehearse it.** You mustn't reach a point where you are so familiar with your speech that you are becoming tired of it, or you will be both bored and boring on the day, and your listeners will be bored, too. No matter how many times you practise it, your speech has to sound fresh at the reception. You may have heard it twenty, thirty, fifty times already, but to your listeners it should sound as if you are making that speech for the very first time.

> Rehearse till you are confident, rehearse till you are satisfied, but *don't* rehearse till you hate the speech.

At the reception: some dos and don'ts

- Unless you are a non-drinker, you will doubtless have a drink or two during the reception, but don't forget that you have to make a speech after the meal, so don't overdo it. If you feel you *have* drunk too much alcohol, and are aware that you might be a little wobbly on your feet or that your voice might be a little shaky or slurred, do something about it quickly: ask for a cup (or a pot!) of coffee.

- If you are nervous, don't make the mistake of thinking that more alcohol will help. It won't. An excess of alcohol might make you *think* you are making a brilliant speech, but you won't be.

Troubleshooting: a speaker has had too much to drink

What should happen if one of the main speakers, through nerves or inattention, gets into an alcoholic state that renders them speechless, or at least hardly fit to speak?

Prevention should be the first objective – if you notice that one of the other scheduled speakers is drinking more than is wise during the meal, have a quick and discreet word with them.

If that doesn't work, there is going to have to be a very quick Plan B. Can you simply drop the speech? It's difficult to do that if it is one of the three key speeches. Is there another family member or friend who could step in at very short notice? If so, don't wait till the last minute – approach them at once, because they are going to need time to get their thoughts in order. If the groom is going to be unable to speak, could the bride do it? If not, it might be down to the best man to say something on the groom's behalf.

Whatever the solution, make light of the situation. The stand-in speaker should give a brief apology and explanation (the situation will be pretty obvious to everyone in any case), and then get on with the speech/toast.

If there is a master or mistress of ceremonies to introduce the speeches, make sure that they know what is going on and who they are to introduce.

- Don't smoke, chew gum, or eat while you are speaking.

- Make sure you have your notes with you and flick through them quickly to make sure the cards are in the correct order. (Remember, you should have numbered them, so it should be easy to check they are all there and in the right order.)

- If you are planning on using any props (see page 43), make sure you have them with you and that they are in working order.

Troubleshooting: no notes, no visual aids

If you have forgotten to bring your speech notes with you, or mislaid them somewhere, then quickly fetch the photocopied version which you will, of course, have left somewhere safe but accessible, for example in your car.

If you have lost your visual aids, or they don't work properly, this may be more of a problem. If you can replace them quickly, then you can carry on as planned. If you can't replace them, you will either have to alter or drop that part of your speech, or admit to your listeners that you had intended to do such-and-such at this point but can't because you have lost your visual aids or because they aren't working. (If they have been mislaid, someone else may perhaps have seen them and will know where they are, and with a short delay you will be able to carry on as planned.)

- It is a good idea to have a glass of water beside you so that you can take a sip from time to time if your mouth becomes dry while you're speaking. (Taking a sip of water also gives you something to do while you are waiting for the room to settle again after that great joke you are going to tell.)

- If you are going to propose a toast, make sure your wine glass has something in it *before* you stand up to speak. (Probably no one would notice if you drank a toast with an empty glass, but you might feel a bit silly.) Alternatively, at the end of your speech, before proposing the toast, you could pause and fill your own glass (make sure the wine bottle is within reach), as this gives everyone else a moment to check whether their glasses are empty and to fill them if need be:

And so, ladies and gentlemen [fill your glass], *I'd like you all to join me now in a toast to the bride and groom.* [Brief pause while people pick up their glasses and stand up.] *John and Julie. May they have a long and happy marriage.*

- If you are speaking where you have been sitting, move your chair back far enough so that you are not jammed against the table. Give yourself room to move.

- There will always be some noise between speeches – people talking, laughing, coughing, moving their seats to get more comfortable, etc. If there is a master or mistress of ceremonies, they will (or should) pause before announcing the next speaker. If there is no MC, you should stand up ready to speak, and then give everyone a few moments to quieten down; don't try to talk over the noise. Use the time while people are settling down again to get settled yourself. Take a few deep breaths to relax.

Troubleshooting: last-minute nerves

What to do if you get a serious attack of nerves at the last minute? If you are well prepared, it probably won't happen, but you need to be ready just in case it does. Make a two-pronged attack, on both the cause of your nerves and the symptoms.

Cause: You're nervous because you're going to have to stand up and speak to a large gathering of people, some of whom you don't know and don't know you.

Cure: Remind yourself that you are talking to friends, whether or not you actually know them. They're all on your side. They're not expecting more of you than are able to give. Your speech is prepared, you've rehearsed it, and it's fine. You know it's fine. And every word you have to say is there in front of you in your notes. Remind yourself also that even experienced public speakers can feel a little nervous before making a speech – it's perfectly natural – but once you are on your feet you'll be too busy speaking to feel nervous about it.

Symptoms: Your mouth will probably be dry. Your heart will be thumping and you will be breathing too fast and shallowly. You may be sweating. Your legs may be shaking.

Cures: If your mouth is dry, sip some water from your glass. Don't take large gulps, just small sips, and swirl the water round your mouth before swallowing it, so that the whole of your mouth is refreshed.

Take some slow, deep breaths (as discreetly as possible): breathe in through your nose while you count to five, pause, and then slowly breathe out again through your mouth while again you count to five, then pause again; repeat the cycle several times. This should stop your heart racing. Another relaxation technique is to clench your fists (do this under the table or people might get the wrong idea!) and then slowly release and stretch your fingers.

If your legs are shaking, press your feet gently but firmly into the floor, and then release them again. Repeat several times.

If you are sweating, quickly wipe the sweat off your face before you stand up (then put your handkerchief away).

There's no avoiding it – you are going to have to stand up sometime. When you do, pause for a moment, get yourself into a comfortable position, take another sip of water, look around at your audience, and *smile*. You may not feel like smiling, but force yourself. It will actually help you relax. Make eye contact with someone (but don't stare).

If you are nervous, you may speak too quickly, or your voice may be strangulated or squeaky. If this happens, stop briefly and take a deep breath before continuing. To avoid embarrassment, you could make a joke of it:

Sorry. I realise I'm speaking too fast. It's just that I know that [the next speaker] has written a great speech and I can't wait to hear what he/she is going to say. Anyhow, as I was trying to say . . .

> *Sorry. I realise I'm speaking too fast, but I know that some of the guys here are anxious to see the bar open and I don't want to keep them waiting.*
>
> *Well, that was my Mickey Mouse/Donald Duck impersonation. Now I'll get on with my speech.*

- Don't loosen your tie and unbutton your collar. Don't take your jacket off unless the room is very warm and others have done so (though if they are wearing morning coats or dinner jackets, they really should not have taken them off at this point, even if they are feeling hot).

- Stick to the basic plan of your speech, but be flexible and don't be afraid to add something in if occurs to you, or you need to respond to something a previous speaker has said. But if you do add something new to your speech, be brief, and don't waffle.

Troubleshooting: offensive ad-libs

Be very careful if you ad-lib in your speech. It is so easy in the heat of the moment to think of this killer one-liner that you add in because it seems a good idea at the time – only to realise as it passes your lips that you have made a *huge* mistake. You can't take it back, and everyone has heard you say it.

You must make an immediate apology:

> *I'm sorry. I realise that that was a stupid thing for me to have said. It was an off-the-cuff remark and I apologise to anyone who found it offensive. From here on, I'll keep to what I have written in front of me.*

Then go on with your speech: the damage is done, but you have done your best to make amends. If there is someone in particular you know you have offended, see them afterwards and apologise again.

- Respond to your listeners' reaction. If you get a laugh at a joke, wait for the laughter to die down before continuing.

Troubleshooting

It would be foolish to worry too much about what could go wrong with your speech, as on most occasions nothing does. Nevertheless, forewarned is forearmed, so here are a few more possible problems and how to deal with them.

• Noise

There are any number of unpredictable ways in which your speech might be interrupted by noise. At many weddings, children's entertainment is provided to keep the children occupied after the meal, but this may not be the case at 'your' wedding. (It might be worth suggesting it, though. The idea may not have occurred to anyone else.) Hopefully, parents will either keep their children quiet during the speeches or take them out if they become too noisy. If they don't, you'll just have to talk over them. You could make a joke about it, for example that it will be their turn to make a speech when they're older, but it's your turn now.

If someone falls asleep during your speech, ignore them (unless you can quickly think of a witty and *inoffensive* remark:

Charlie read over my speech last night and it was so boring he's obviously decided to sleep through it today.

If the sleeper is snoring, someone sitting close to them will surely wake them up.

If noise from outside the room threatens to drown out your words, make a joke of it if you can. If it is the noise of a police car, for example:

I know this speech is really criminal, but I didn't think anyone would actually call the police.

If it is a fire brigade siren:

I thought there was a funny smell coming from the kitchen.

If it is just general traffic noise:

It's no good trying to drown me out – I spent ages writing this speech and I'm going to get through it right, reason or none.

If a bell rings:

Is that someone telling me my time is up?

If the noise does drown you out, however, just stop until it is over.

• No one laughs at your joke

What do you do if your joke falls flat? One thing *not* to do is to pause too long waiting for the laugh to come: all you'll get is an embarrassed silence or forced laughter. If everyone has missed the point, or didn't find the remark funny, just keep going.

Alternatively, you could make a joke of it yourself, which usually gets a laugh and saves any embarrassment:

You may laugh. Well, at least you were meant to at that point . . .

or:

It says here in my notes 'Pause for laughter'. Well, I hope I don't have to wait too long, or we'll never get the dancing started.

• Hecklers

It is perhaps worth giving some thought to how to handle a heckler, though it is not a likely occurrence at a wedding reception. If anyone interrupts your speech, it will generally be with good-humoured banter. Whether you respond to it, and how, depends on how quickly you can think on your feet. You could make a play of taking out a pencil, and jotting down something on your speech notes, saying:

> *Thanks. I'll use that one the next time I have to make a speech.*

Or you could say:

> *Sorry, I haven't got time to answer questions.*

A technique used by some comedians who work in clubs is to pretend not to hear what the heckler has said and make them say it two or three times; nothing is ever so funny or clever when it is repeated.

If the heckling becomes offensive, and the heckler just won't stop, don't get into an argument and don't make fun of the heckler, or you may make a bad situation worse. Someone sitting nearby will almost certainly come to your aid and tell the heckler to be quiet, or usher them out of the room. As a last resort, give in if you can't win:

> *Well, it's clear I'm not going to manage to say anything more, so I'll just stop here and ask you all to join with me in wishing . . .*

You get the Brownie points for staying calm, and everyone's sympathy for having your speech disrupted; the heckler gets hell for the rest of the evening.

If you are in a public restaurant, making a short speech or proposing a toast, and someone else, not one of your party, starts to make comments, what should you do?

If the outsider is clearly just joining in in the spirit of the occasion, a little banter to and fro does no harm at all, so long as it doesn't get out of hand and doesn't annoy other diners. If you think it *is* getting out of hand or annoying other people, then try to withdraw politely, for example saying that while you are enjoying the fun, you don't want to disturb the other diners too much and think you should stop. You could drink a quick toast to the outsider's health, and then pointedly, but not rudely, turn back to your own group. If necessary, sit down and continue what you were saying quietly so that you are not attracting quite so much attention.

If the outsider doesn't take the hint, or is heckling you or making inappropriate remarks, or is expressing objections to what you are doing (whether or not you think they are justified), don't get into an argument. If you are clearly being a nuisance to others (in their opinion, even if not in yours), stop, apologise, and sit down. You can always propose your toast quietly, while remaining seated, when the situation has calmed down. If, on the other hand, it is the other diner who is causing a disruption, let the restaurant manager or staff deal with it. That is their job; it is not yours.

Microphones

At most wedding receptions, a microphone won't be necessary. Even if one is made available, you may not need it (so don't feel you have to use it if you don't want to). The microphone may be on a stand, or you may have to hold it.

It is unlikely you will have a chance to try out speaking with the microphone before the reception itself, so here are some useful tips:

- If there is a microphone, make sure you know how to operate it. Find out before it is time to speak.

- If the microphone is on a stand, make sure it is at a comfortable height for you to speak into. You don't want to be stretching up while you speak, nor do you want to be bending over it.

- If the microphone is on a stand, don't stand too close to it; if you are holding it, don't hold it too close to your mouth. There should be about four inches between the microphone and your mouth.

- Don't speak too loudly into it. It's there so that you *don't* have to shout. Just speak normally. From the first couple of sentences you speak, judge how loud your voice has to be to be heard, and adjust your volume accordingly.

- Keep the microphone well away from the food and drink during the meal.

- Don't switch it on until you are ready to use it. (Remember the many radio and TV personalities and politicians who have been caught out making injudicious remarks when they thought their microphone was switched off.)

Troubleshooting: feedback

If you get feedback (a howling or squealing noise caused by the sound coming out of the loudspeakers being fed back into the sound system through the microphone again), there should be someone in charge who can sort out the problem. (Check in advance that this will be the case.) But if there is no one to help you, then try moving slightly closer to the microphone. If that doesn't help, you may have to change your position completely: the loudspeakers should be further forward than the microphone and pointing away from it, so if you can't move them, move yourself and the microphone to a better position.

7 The father of the bride

Let's begin by setting out the main elements of the father of the bride's speech (though not necessarily in the order you will want them in your speech):

- You welcome the guests and thank them for coming. You should mention the groom's parents and close family by name, and any other special guests.

- You may also want to pick out for particular mention and thanks any relatives or guests who have come a long way or who have had to make a special effort to get to the wedding.

- You might also mention any relatives or friends of either family who are not able to be with you, for example due to illness, and express hopes for their recovery (or whatever the circumstances require). Check beforehand with the groom's family whether there is anyone they would like you to mention.

- It might be appropriate to mention at this point a relative or friend who would have been at the wedding but who sadly has died. (There is no reason not to mention the deceased at a wedding – their presence will be missed, and it is right not to ignore this. It will cast a slight shadow over the celebrations for a moment, but you can lift everyone's spirits again with the rest of your speech.)

- You will say how proud you and your wife are of your daughter, perhaps with a mention of any of her notable achievements, and you might congratulate the groom on his choice of wife. You will of course say how beautiful she looks. And at some point you should also say something complimentary about the bridesmaid – especially if she's your daughter too!

- You will probably relate one or two amusing or interesting stories about events in your daughter's life or about aspects of her character.

- You should say a few complimentary words about the groom, and how happy you and your wife are that your daughter has chosen such a fine husband. What was your reaction when you first met him? If you can think of an amusing way of completing it, there is no harm in using the old chestnut 'I've not so not so much lost a daughter as gained a . . .'.

- You will say how happy you and your family have been to get to know the groom's family.

- You may have an amusing story to tell about something that happened during the wedding preparations.

- Since as the father of the bride you are the host at the reception, and everyone has (hopefully!) just enjoyed an excellent meal, you may want to include a word of thanks to the caterers. Also to anyone else who has played a part in the wedding preparations, the ceremony (especially the minister), or the reception.

- You may tell a joke or two, or another amusing story.

- You might include a few words of advice – tongue-in-cheek or serious – to the newly-weds as they start out on their life together. If it's serious advice, don't labour the point.

- Finally you will bring your speech to a close by inviting everyone present to join you in toasting the bride and groom.

A sample speech

[Addressing the audience]
Well, everyone,

[Amusing introduction]

We've all enjoyed an excellent meal, I think, and I'm afraid this is where you pay for it! I don't mean I'll be passing round the hat. It's even worse than that. You have to listen to me making a speech. Perhaps some of you would prefer it if I just passed round the hat!

[The welcomes]

First of all, although I think I have actually spoken to all of you already this afternoon before the meal, I'd like on behalf of Mary and myself to welcome you here once more, and to thank you all for coming and sharing this special day with us.

I want to say a particular word of welcome to Tom and Joyce, John's mum and dad. It's been a privilege and a pleasure to get to know them over the past few months, and again I speak for both Mary and myself when I say that in Tom and Joyce we have gained not just two new relatives but two good friends, and we are looking forward to seeing a lot more of them in the future.

I know that many of you have travelled long distances to be with us today, but I hope none of you will be offended if I say a special thank you to Bob and Barbara who have come all the way from New Zealand especially to attend Julie and John's wedding. I'm glad to say that they had a safe and uneventful journey here, and I'm sure you will all join with me in wishing them an equally safe and uneventful flight home again, though they aren't leaving immediately – they'll be spending the next three weeks with us and visiting as many members of the English branch of the family as they can while they're over here (or should that be 'up here'?).

[Change of subject: your daughter]

Well, anyway. One of the pleasures in life for a father is that he gets to say a few words about his daughter when she gets married. To sing her praises, of course, and perhaps to embarrass her just a little! When I sat down a few weeks ago to write this speech, so many memories came to mind that I could hardly get them down on paper fast enough. I thought back to the tiny baby I held in my arms in the hospital (in absolute terror of dropping her!) and how I wondered at that moment who she would take after – she did look a bit like Winston Churchill at the time. I tried to picture what she would look like as a girl, and as a grown woman, and then I looked at Julie's mother lying half-asleep on the bed beside us and I knew for sure that Julie would grow into the beauty that she is today.

I remembered the day Julie took her first step. I remembered her first day at school: she was so eager to learn, and I remembered her tears of disappointment when she came back from school that lunchtime, still not able to read and write! I remembered her in her first party dress, and on the beach in her first bikini. So many memories, so many firsts. I could stand here all evening talking about them.

[Lead into an anecdote]

I well remember Julie's first word: it was 'dog'. Julie has always loved dogs. Even as a toddler she had no fear of them, not even ones that were twice her size and hit her in the face with their tails. In fact, as many of you will already know, Julie has always had a fondness for 'all creatures great and small'. I'll not talk about some of the small ones she kept in her bedroom, or unfortunately didn't manage to keep in her bedroom – I can still see the look of horror on Mary's elderly aunt's face as she watched a snail climbing up the table cloth as we sat down to tea one Sunday evening. We coped better with the bigger animals, though. As a little girl, Julie pestered us and pestered us till we bought her a dog, and then of course, one dog wasn't enough; she had to have two. And then she wanted a cat. And then a rabbit. After a trip to the zoo, when she was about seven, I think, she thought it would be nice to have a hippopotamus, but her mother and I drew the line at that – we told her the bath wasn't big enough!

[Lead from anecdotes into a joke]

Talking of Julie and her love of animals puts me in mind of a joke. Don't stop me if you've heard it because it's the only one I know.

[Tell a suitable joke]

[From joke back to daughter again]

I suppose with her love of animals, it was only to be expected that Julie would become a vet when she grew up. For Mary and me, it was one of the proudest moments in our lives when we watched Julie graduate two years ago. And we were delighted when she got a job in a veterinary practice not far from here.

[Lead on to groom]

Beauty, kindness, a loving heart, intelligence, and a successful career. What more could a father want for his daughter? Well, I suppose one other thing any father would wish for his daughter is to see her happily married. And you have only got to look at Julie and John together to see how happily married she is. Are marriages made in heaven? This one certainly is. We've known John now for almost two years, and we couldn't imagine a better man to be with Julie for the rest of her life. I know it's an old and hackneyed cliché to say that we have not so much lost a daughter as gained a son, but in John's case that is exactly how it feels. While officially I may have 'given Julie away' this afternoon, in reality it is not Julie who has left our family through her marriage today, but John who has finally become the son that Mary and I have long considered him to be.

[The grand finale]

John and I have enjoyed many chats together over the past couple of years, about life, about politics, about football, about Julie. But we haven't talked much about marriage. So this afternoon, as a man who has had a long and happy married life, I want to finish here by giving John just one word of advice: remember that all any woman asks of her husband is that he should love her – and obey all her commandments!

[The toast]

And now I'd like to ask everyone to join me in a toast to Julie and John, the bride and groom. May the worst day of their future be better than the best day of their past!

Julie and John.

If there are children of the bride and/or groom

Any children of the bride and groom should be brought into the speech at some point:

> *Now it is often said that the only reason for going through the trauma of bringing up children is so that you can have grandchildren! And as you all know, now that Rosemary and Michael are married, I find myself not only a father-in-law to Michael but also a grandfather to his two lovely children, Lucy and Kevin, who are sitting here with us at the table, and are probably hoping that I stop talking soon but are too polite to say so.*

They may also be mentioned in the toast:

> *And now I'd like to ask everyone to join me in a toast to Rosemary and Michael, and Lucy and Kevin, as they start out on their new life together. May the worst day of their future together be better than the best day of their past!*
>
> *Rosemary and Michael, and Lucy and Kevin.*

The substitute speaker

If you are speaking in place of the bride's father, what you say in your speech will obviously depend on the circumstances. If the bride's father is dead, guests are likely to be aware of this already. If he has suddenly been taken ill, however, and you are standing in at the last minute, many of the guests may not be aware of the circumstances.

Whatever the situation, it is best that you make some comment about it. If the bride's father is dead, you could say you know how proud he was of his daughter and how proud he would have been to walk down the aisle with her. If he is alive, but unable to attend, you could say much the same thing, but of course add reassurances that he is recovering, or express hopes for his speedy recovery. If he was supposed to be at the wedding but has been delayed en route, it would again be better to explain what has happened.

In all these cases, you should also say that you are pleased and honoured to have been asked to stand in to make the speech, and express the hope that you will do it as well as the father would have done.

If the father of the bride is dead, it would be customary to say a few words about him:

> *Of course, as you all know, it should be Julie's dad making this speech this afternoon, not me. I was very honoured when Julie asked me to speak, and I know that Julie and Mary would like me to say just a few words about Dave this afternoon.*

After some suitable words about the bride's father, you would then go on to say what a credit the bride is to her father, etc., before moving on to the speech itself by welcoming the guests.

If the bride's father and mother are divorced, and the bride's father is not at the wedding, it is probably better not to mention him at all. Have someone announce you so that everyone knows who you are, and just get on with the speech.

8 The bridegroom

The bridegroom speaks mostly on behalf of his wife and himself, but of course, if he talks to or about his bride, he speaks for himself alone. (And if the bride is going to make a speech of her own, she and the groom will have agreed beforehand who is going to say what. Perhaps it is the bride who will propose a toast to her bridesmaid, rather than the bridegroom, as is traditional.)

The easiest way for the groom to begin his speech is by thanking the father of the bride for his kind words and the toast he has just proposed. This both links his speech to what has gone before and also provides a lead-in to what he should say next.

You might want to work in 'My wife and I' at some point in your speech; it will of course be met with cheers and/or groans.

The bridegroom's speech should (or could) include the following:

- Thank the bride's parents for welcoming you into the family, and for allowing you to marry their daughter (though only if this is appropriate – for example, if the bride and groom have already been living together for a number of years, the bride's father's permission for the marriage is unlikely to have been asked for, and a modern bride may consider that her father has no right to any say in whom she marries anyway).

- Thank the bride's father for the wedding and the reception (if he is paying for it), perhaps also adding your and your wife's thanks to the caterers (if they deserve it).

- Thank the guests for attending the wedding, for their good wishes, and for their gifts; there might be a mention here of anyone who has not been able to come (depending on what has already been said by the father of the bride and what is going to be said by the best man).

- Thank the person who performed the wedding ceremony (if appropriate – you would not normally thank a registrar, but you should certainly thank the minister/priest/rabbi, etc., whether or not they are at the reception).

- Thank the best man and the ushers for their help and support (there is scope for a joke or two there); if the best man is not a close relative of yours, you may at this point make some remarks about how you met and became friends, with a suitable story or two (also admitting facetiously that you are a little worried about what stories the best man is going to tell about you!).

- Thank any other helpers (e.g. the organist, the bell-ringers, the friend who sang at the wedding ceremony, or the friend who videoed it).

- Thank your new wife for agreeing to marry you, and how fortunate you are to have such a beautiful/intelligent/successful/understanding/loving bride, perhaps including a word or two of praise and thanks to her parents for how they have brought her up. (At this point you may be addressing your remarks directly to your bride, not the guests, so look at her, not at them.)

- Thank your own parents for how they have brought you up, and for their support and guidance through the years.

- Thank the bridesmaid on your wife's behalf for her help and support (unless the bride is going to say that herself in her own speech), not forgetting to mention pageboys and flower girls if there are any.

A large part of the bridegroom's speech involves saying thank you, but just as with the father of the bride's speech, there should be some lighter moments. The bridegroom should include the story of how he and his wife met, perhaps with an amusing anecdote about how their relationship developed. There could also be an amusing tale about the wedding preparations.

If the father of the bride has included in his speech some (serious or facetious) advice to the newly-weds, the bridegroom should acknowledge it and if possible respond to it (similarly seriously or facetiously).

It would be good, when saying how lovely his bride looks, if the bridegroom had a word or two of admiration for her mother and any sisters (though the sisters are likely to be bridesmaids, so that can come towards the end of the speech). And having praised the bride's mother and sisters, he must not forget to praise his own!

Some bridegrooms propose a toast to the mothers about here, but since he is going to propose a toast to the bridesmaid in a moment, it is perhaps better left to someone else – the bride could do it in her speech, or the father of the groom could make a short speech later on that ends with a toast to his wife and the bride's mother.

Lastly, the bridegroom's speech should return to the bridesmaid. He has already thanked her for her help on behalf of his wife; now it is his turn to make some complimentary remarks about her, before inviting everyone to join him in a toast to her.

Presentation of gifts

It is normal for the bride and groom to give gifts to the bridesmaid, the best man, etc., to thank them for their help and as a memento of the occasion. This may be done during the bridegroom's speech, at the point where he thanks them. There is much to be said for this, as it is a good way of expressing the couple's thanks publicly, in deed as well as in words. However, on the downside, if several gifts have to be presented, it can be a little disruptive to the speech.

If gifts are only to be presented to one or two bridesmaids and to the best man, all of whom will probably be at the top table with the rest of the wedding party, this can easily be done during the speech with very little fuss. If, however, there are gifts to be given to several bridesmaids, some flower girls and/or pageboys, the best man, and the ushers, most of whom will not be at the top table, presenting the gifts will involve much more to-ing and fro-ing and scraping of seats. It'll end up like a school prizegiving. It might therefore be better if the gifts were simply mentioned at this point but handed out at another time, for example after all the speeches are over.

Alternatively, you could ask the ushers to come to the top table and pick up the gifts, which they then distribute to the others. But be aware that if the gifts are then opened by their recipients, there may be a lot of chatter and laughter which you will have to talk over, or else wait for it to die down before getting people's attention again and resuming your speech. For a little while, you are going to be on your feet with nothing to do.

Many couples also like to present the two mothers with a small gift at the reception. This can be done at the point in the speech where the groom is singing their praises.

How many people do you give special gifts to? Do you need to include sisters, aunts, grandmothers? You and the bride must decide that. Do what you think is appropriate. But here again, the more gifts presented during the speech, the more disruptive the whole process becomes.

A sample speech

[Addressing your audience]
Mum and Dad, Dave and Mary (or maybe I should be calling you 'Mum and Dad' as well now), our family, Julie's family, all our friends, and that couple at the back who I don't recognise and Julie says she's never seen before either,

[Opener]
My wife and I . . . I was told I had to start my speech that way so that you could all cheer and bang on the tables, but in fact I wanted to anyway, because, you know, the most important thing that has ever happened in my life happened to me this afternoon when Julie said 'I do'. I have to admit I was holding my breath at that point, just in case she said, 'No, I don't'!

[Move on to welcomes and thanks]

Now, as the bridegroom, I have a lot of people to thank this after-noon. Firstly, Julie and I, that is 'my wife and I' (there, I've said it again – I really like saying it) want to thank you all for being here with us on this special day, for all your good wishes, and of course for your wonderful gifts. You have been so generous, we were beginning to think we might have to sell our flat and buy a bigger one in order to find space for everything!

[Respond to father of the bride's speech]

Next, I want to thank Dave and Mary and Paul for welcoming me into their family. I'm not sure what they thought of me that first day that Julie took me home, but they certainly made me feel that I was the best thing since sliced bread. (By the way, does anyone know what was the best thing before sliced bread? I've always wondered.) And I must of course thank Dave for his kind words, and for his advice. I think Julie must have had a look at her dad's speech at some point recently, because strangely enough she said the very same thing to me just the other day!

[Thanks to parents]

Of course, it goes without saying, but I'm going to say it anyway, that I owe so much to my mum and dad. They've always been there for me, even at times – especially during my teenage Goth period – when they must have wondered who on earth this creature was that was living in their house with them. Well, turning up for meals, at least. Like many teenagers, I despised my parents' ignor-ance and backward bourgeois tendencies, and certainly didn't want to be seen anywhere in their company, but I still loved my mum's cooking!

[Bring in compliment to the mothers]

And while I'm talking about my mother, I just want to say how stun-ning both my mum and Julie's mum look this afternoon. Don't you agree? And aren't those hats fantastic!

[Thanks to best man and ushers]

Now, who else have I got to thank? Chris, of course, for being my best man, and George, Guy and Eddie for agreeing to act as ushers. We go back a long way together. We were the gang who set out to rival the Secret Seven (though there were only five of us, and we didn't allow girls in). We were at school together, though our teachers soon realised that classes were less disrupted if we were actually kept apart! These guys were my fellow Goths in our teenage years. And although we have gone our separate ways since our schooldays, we have always kept in touch, and I know we always will. There's a bond between us that will never be broken. I was going to talk about some of our adventures together, but I think I'll leave that to Chris. He says he has some cracking stories to tell about me.

[More thanks]

So passing quickly on, because I can see some people looking at their watches, and there's one gentleman over there shaking his watch vigorously to see if it is still working, I want to thank Mr Green for conducting such a beautiful wedding ceremony this afternoon, and for the wise words of advice he gave us in his sermon. And although she is not here with us, we must of course also thank Mrs Garrett for playing the organ for us.

As Dave has already said, we have all enjoyed an excellent meal here this afternoon, and I think it only right that we should thank the staff of the hotel for their important contribution to the success of the day. The chicken chasseur was almost as good as my mother's!

[Thanks and compliments to bride]

Most important of all, as I'm sure you'll agree, I want to thank Julie for agreeing to marry me. As her father said, she's beautiful, she's intelligent, she's kind, she's loving, and even now, after the ceremony this afternoon, I can still hardly believe that she has become my wife.

[Turn to toast the bride]
Julie, my darling, someone once said that a good marriage is not a matter of finding the right partner but of being the right partner. But I think it's both. I know that in you I have found the person I want to spend the rest of my life with, and I promise you that I will do everything I can, every day, to be the right partner for you. And as a token of this promise, I want to drink this toast to you. To Julie, the love of my life.

[Turn back to the guests for the compliments to the bridesmaid]
Normally the bridegroom finishes his speech by proposing a toast to the bridesmaid, and my speech will be no exception. What can I say about Emma? She has been such a help to Julie, and to me, over the past months, always there with wise advice, practical suggestions, and many a bottle of wine. She looks so dainty and delicate sitting there in her bridesmaid's dress, but I can assure you she is one strong-minded girl and when tempers got a bit frayed over the past few months, as I'm afraid they occasionally did, she was well able to bang our heads together (fortunately not literally!) till we saw sense. I don't know how we would have managed without her.

[On to the toast]
And so ladies and gentlemen, friends, family, I would like you all to join with me now in a toast to our beautiful bridesmaid Emma.
    To Emma.

9 The best man

The best man's speech is usually expected to be the highlight of the three speeches (so no pressure there, then), not because he is more important than the other two speakers, but because they have done most of the serious work (the main welcomes and thank yous) and the best man is therefore free to deliver a more light-hearted and entertaining speech, with jokes and funny stories and, of course, amusing (but not *too* embarrassing) anecdotes about the bridegroom. What the best man can say in his speech also depends on his relationship to the groom's family: a best man who is part of the family, say the bridegroom's brother, can perhaps say things that a best man who is only a friend of the bridegroom can't.

Throughout this book, it is assumed for the sake of convenience that the best man is male, but it is becoming quite common nowadays for a female friend or relative of the groom to be invited to be his 'best man' (or 'best woman', or simply the 'bridegroom's attendant'). While the best man is always referred to in this book as 'he', everything that is said about a male best man applies equally well to a female best man (except perhaps the sort of anecdote she tells!).

The following are the main elements of the best man's speech:

- You might start your speech by introducing yourself (if you are not the groom's brother, for example, some of the guests might like to know how you and the groom became friends), and saying why you think you were chosen to be the best man.

- You reply on behalf of the bridesmaid to the toast made by the bridegroom at the end of his speech (unless she is going to do this herself);

if the groom has included flower girls and pageboys in his speech (as he should have), you include them in your thanks. This part of the speech should also include or be followed by your own complimentary remarks about her/them. If the bride and groom have given the bridesmaid, etc. gifts for their services, you say thank you for these as well.

- You acknowledge the groom's thanks to yourself and the ushers (and the gifts you have received if they have been handed out by this time), and say what a pleasure and honour it has been to be the best man. Since the ushers have been your assistants throughout the day, you thank them for their help, with special mention of the chief usher, who has been your deputy.

- You might want to thank the caterers for their efficient service (if it has been – but if it hasn't, it's better to say nothing); if no one else has done so, you should thank the minister/registrar for their help (even if they are not present at the reception) and similarly the church caretaker, organist, etc. who have contributed to the success of the day. You may also have been asked by the bride or groom to make a special mention of someone or other they want to thank (though the bride's father or the groom could do this in their speeches).

- Check with the bride and groom if there is anything you should say, anyone you should mention. Ask the groom if there is anything special he intends to say about the bridesmaid, so that you can respond to it when you speak on her behalf.

- You may, on your own behalf and on behalf of the guests, thank the bride's parents for the reception.

- You congratulate the bride and groom, expressing your good wishes for their future happiness, and of course make some complimentary remarks about the lovely bride and the groom's good luck in persuading her to marry him.

- You might compliment the mothers of the bride and groom.

- Tell some amusing and embarrassing tales about the groom, and also include some stories showing his good side; like the other speakers, you can add in some other jokes and amusing stories.

- At the end of your speech, you read out the messages from well-wishers who are not at the wedding.

A key point to note is that **you do *not* toast the bride and groom** (a common mistake). The toast to the bride and groom has already been proposed by the father of the bride. You do, of course, express your good wishes for their future happiness, but you do not call on everyone else to join you in a toast to them.

You probably do not propose any toast at all at the end of your speech. However, you may want to, or be asked to, propose a toast to the bride's parents as hosts of the wedding and the reception; or, after reading out the cards and letters from well-wishers, you may propose a toast to 'absent friends'. This is something you will have discussed with the bride and groom beforehand.

Well-wishers' messages

When you have a moment before the meal, gather together all the cards, letters, telemessages, etc., that have been sent to the bride and groom or their families by friends and relatives who are not attending the wedding. (The groom should already have given you any that he has received, and you should have reminded the bride's and groom's parents to bring the ones that they have received. Remember that some messages may have been sent directly to the reception venue, so ask the staff for these, too.)

You should try to read over all the messages before (or, if necessary, even during) the meal to make sure you can read the handwriting and decipher the signatures (ask a member of each family to help if you can't). You may want to note anything that is not suitable for reading out, and decide how you will cut down messages that are very long (people sometimes include poetry or literary passages with their congratulations, but reading it all out might make the reading of the messages take longer than desirable – and the poetry is often pretty awful anyway). The bride and groom and their families can read all the cards and letters again later on, including the bits you have missed out.

It is also important to check that all the messages are appropriate for reading out to a group that may include elderly people and children: for example, the message from the lads in the rugby club might have made them laugh, and might make you and the groom laugh, but it might offend some of the guests. Make a joke of it:

> *And finally, there is a message here from the lads in the rugby club that, since there are children present, I am not going to read out. I don't want to have to explain the joke. Worse still, kids being what they are today, I might not have to! If anyone wants to read this card, see me afterwards.*

You can, of course, create some spoof messages to read out. For example, what do you think some well-known female film/sports/TV personality would say if they had just found out that the love of their life (the bridegroom) was getting married? Or what advice would some male film/sports/TV personality send to the bridegroom on his wedding day?

Troubleshooting: missing messages

If either father has forgotten the cards and letters, and if there is still time to fetch them, find out where they are and send someone for them. Otherwise, either ignore the problem and simply read the cards and letters you have (which may make one family wonder why Great-aunt Jean in Australia didn't send a message) or admit that the cards have been left behind (which may embarrass the father concerned). Discuss with said father which he would prefer.

When you read out the congratulatory messages, speak clearly and slowly (just as you did when making the speech) and pause between reading each one, as the families and guests may be laughing at what you have just read out, or commenting on it to each other. Don't try to talk over the noise.

Announcements

It is sometimes suggested that, at the end of his speech, the best man should announce the programme for the rest of the evening. You *can* do this, but again you should not do so if there are other speeches to follow, because that would interrupt the smooth flow from one to the next. It is far better to wait until all the speeches are over before any announcements are made. And even if the best man's speech is the last one, it is perhaps better for there to be a short interval to allow the families and guests to chat about the speeches, the well-wishers' messages, etc. before you try to draw everyone's attention to other matters.

If there is an MC, the programme for the rest of the evening can be announced by them, along with any other necessary announcements.

If your speech is the last one, and there is no MC, it should be you who announces that the bride and groom will now cut the wedding cake. If there are speeches to follow yours, the cake is not cut until they are all over, at which point either you or the MC will announce the cutting of the cake.

A sample speech

[Addressing the audience]
Well, everyone.

[The opener]
Since there is no master of ceremonies this afternoon, and I was given the job of introducing the speakers, I now have great pleasure in calling on myself to give the best man's speech.

[Introduction, with anecdotes]

Now some of you may be wondering who I am, and why John asked me to be his best man. I can tell you that Julie and Emma have frequently asked John over the past few months why on earth he asked me to be his best man!

As John has told you, we have been friends for a long time now. We were in the same class at school, and I think we actually became friends because he knew I had more comics than he had and I knew that if I gave him one of my comics he'd let me copy his homework. I don't know how he explained all those comics to his mum and dad over the years, but he no doubt came up with some plausible story, because he's always been able to talk his way out of trouble. We used to call him Mr Blarney.

But John's not only very good at talking himself out of difficult situations, he's also very good at talking people into things. But one thing John didn't have to talk me into was being his best man. I was really delighted and honoured to be asked, though a bit surprised because John must know some of the stories I could tell you this afternoon. There are some things even Julie doesn't know about him yet! But it's not too late, John. Twenty pounds, and my lips are sealed – and my speech will be a lot shorter, too!

[Joke]

In a way, though, I do feel a bit of a fraud being called the 'best man', because clearly the best man here today is not me, but John. Well, if he isn't, I don't know why Julie's marrying him. Surely she isn't settling for second best, is she?

[Reply on behalf of bridesmaid]

Now I've actually never been to a wedding before, and I didn't have much of a clue about what a best man was supposed to say in his speech, apart from taking the mickey out of the bridegroom. I found out that the best man should speak for the bridesmaid and thank the bridegroom for his kind words to her and his toast, but Emma has said that she would prefer to do that for herself, and we'll be hearing from her shortly. So, back to John.

[Joke at bridegroom's expense]
As many of you will know, John's a great Arsenal supporter, and he actually wanted to wear his Arsenal shirt to the wedding instead of the traditional morning coat. Julie was, of course, dead set against this, so the guy at the dress-hire shop suggested that John should do what Julie wanted, but put 'Arsenal' on the back of the morning coat in big letters to show which team he supports. We tried it out, but we found that there was only enough space on the jacket for the first four letters. I thought it looked OK myself, but John wasn't very happy with it.

[Follow-on joke]
Talking about Arsenal reminds me of a joke I heard recently. Two [name a team] *fans once went on a weekend fishing trip to Scotland. Late on the Saturday afternoon they were out on a boat in the middle of a loch, when suddenly one of them looked at his watch and burst into tears.*

'What's wrong?' said his friend.

'[The team] have just lost again,' wept the first man.

'Now, look, don't be silly,' said his friend. 'We're out here, in the middle of a loch, in the middle of nowhere. How on earth can you possibly know that [the team] have lost the game today?'

The first man pointed to his watch. 'It's quarter to five.'

[A semi-serious bit]
People often ask me when I knew that it was getting serious between John and Julie. I can remember the day exactly. It was a Saturday and Arsenal were playing at home. And John announced that, no, he wasn't coming to the match that afternoon; he was going shopping – with some girl called Julie! Shopping? On a Saturday afternoon? With a girl? There had to be something special going on. And of

*course, when I was eventually allowed to meet Julie – and John kept
the two of us apart for quite a long time – I could see at once why
football had taken second place in his life.*

[Compliments to the bride]
*We've heard both John and Dave say what a wonderful girl Julie is,
and I can't think of anything I could add to what they have said. I've
known Julie now for nearly two years, and I can say that John is a
very lucky man. I've sometimes thought that if I had met Julie first,
John might have been standing here today as my best man, but I
know that isn't so: since they met, Julie has only had eyes for John –
well, and Brad Pitt and Leonardo DiCaprio, but they don't count,
do they?*

[Another joke]
*Now I've talked a lot about football, but I wouldn't want you all to
think that that's John's only interest in life (other than Julie). There's
beer as well! Actually, not many people know this, but John has
donated his body to medical science, and he's agreed to preserve it in
alcohol till they're ready to use it!*

[Thanks to the ushers]
*Mentioning alcohol brings me, for some reason, to the ushers. John
has already thanked George, Guy and Eddie for their assistance this
afternoon, and I just want to say a word of thanks to them too. They
did a marvellous job directing the traffic outside and inside the
church and keeping everyone dry during that sudden downpour.
And don't they look smart! I don't think I've seen the three of them in
suits and respectable haircuts since that day they appeared in court.
Only joking!*

[Come to a close]
*Well, I think I have spoken long enough, and I know I have one more
duty to perform, which is to read out the letters and cards that have*

*come from people who are unable to be with us today. So, here's the
first card, with a rather willowy bride on it, and it reads . . .*

You may have been asked to follow the reading of the well-wishers' messages by proposing a toast to 'absent friends'. If so, something along these lines would be appropriate:

*Well, that's the last of the cards and letters, ladies and gentlemen.
Now, as we are remembering all these friends and relatives who are
not able to be here with us today, and knowing that they will be
thinking of us too, especially John and Julie, Dave and Mary, and
Tom and Joyce, I would like you all to join with me now in drinking
a toast.*

To absent friends. Near or far, they are always close to our hearts.

10 The bride and bridesmaid

Traditionally, neither the bride nor the bridesmaid make a speech at a wedding. But at present-day weddings, it is quite normal for a bride to say a few words on her own behalf, and it is not uncommon for the bridesmaid also to make a short speech. We'll look at both these speeches in this chapter.

The bride

Since the bride's speech is not one of the three traditional wedding speeches, there is nothing set down about what should be included. As the bride, you can say whatever you want to say. You and your husband may have agreed in advance that he will cover some subjects and you will cover others (such as thanking the bridesmaid). But keep it fairly short. There have probably been three speakers before you, and no matter how much the guests are enjoying the speeches, there can be too much of a good thing.

If you are the last speaker, you could make a joke about starting off in your marriage the way you intend to continue, by having the last word (but make sure that neither the best man nor the MC is going to use the same joke). Your speech should probably include:

- thanks to your husband for marrying you, probably with an anecdote or two about how you met, what you thought of him, how your relationship developed

- thanks to your in-laws for being so welcoming

- thanks to your bridesmaid for being there for you, possibly with a story of how you met and became friends

A sample speech

[Introduction]
I know that traditionally the bride is expected to let her husband speak on her behalf, but this is the twenty-first century and I think a woman should speak for herself. Anyone who knows me knows that I can talk for Britain, but I'll try not to talk for too long this afternoon, though there are so many things I would love to tell you about my wonderful new husband that I could be on my feet for an hour or more!

[Thanks]
John has already thanked all of you both for your presence here and your presents to us. I don't want to repeat everything he has said, but I do just want to say 'thank you' to all of you for your kindness. John has suggested we might have to move to a bigger flat to accommodate all your gifts, but I can tell you, and him, that since we've just finished decorating the flat we have, we're not moving!

The main reason I want to speak this afternoon, though, is not as an expression of women's lib, but so that I can say a very big thank you to Dave and Mary for welcoming me into their family, and for giving us such a marvellous wedding and reception. I also want to thank them for their part in making John what he is today, and I can assure Mary that I will carry on her good work: I have now reached page sixty-seven of the training manual, though I haven't yet found the page where it tells me how to get him to do the washing up!

I also want to thank my mum and dad and my brother Paul for being the family they are and for showing me what a family should be. They've always backed me in everything I have wanted to do – except for the hippopotamus! – and I know that I owe so much of my success to their support. I certainly don't think I'd have got through my GCSE French without my mum's help!

To Emma, of course, I owe another big thank you for all her help, advice and support. We've known each other since our first day at school and we've been virtually inseparable ever since. We spent so much of our lives together, in and out of each other's houses, that our mothers both thought they had two daughters! Emma and I even went to the same university, so even that didn't separate us. Do you know, the next two weeks, when John and I will be on our honeymoon, will be the most time that Emma and I will have spent apart in the twenty years since we first met. Emma's an amazing girl, and I love her like the sister she virtually is.

[Remarks about husband]

There's one piece of advice that Emma gave me that I'm glad I didn't take. She's not often wrong, but she was wrong about John. Mind you, when I tell you how John and I met, she was right to have misgivings. John and I met on a bus. Nothing odd about that, you may say. I'd seen John on the bus before, but we'd never spoken. Well, this particular evening, he sat down beside me, and before we'd gone two stops he was fast asleep – with his head on my shoulder! And dribbling a bit! I wasn't quite sure what to do, but he seemed harmless. I knew where he was supposed to get off, so I woke him up. Of course, he was so embarrassed, and kept on apologising, and then we got to talking, and I missed my stop too. We eventually got off the bus together, and John asked me if I'd like a coffee. We found a café, and sat over our coffees for hours, just chatting. We found we had so much in common. Eventually the café owners wanted to close up for the night, and we had to leave. John walked me home, asked me out the next night, and gave me a kiss that certainly wasn't appropriate from someone I'd only known for about four hours (not that I was complaining, though!). We've been together ever since, and I just can't imagine life without him.

[Toast to husband]

Since John has toasted me, I think it is only right that I should toast him in return. John, since that day when fate threw us together on the bus and you used me as a pillow, I've been sure that you were the only man for me. Someone once said that love is insanity, and I am certainly madly in love with you! To John, my husband, today, tomorrow, forever!

The bridesmaid

Throughout this book, we have for convenience been talking about 'the bridesmaid', and we shall continue to do so in this chapter. However, as was pointed out before, this is simply a shorthand for 'one or more bridesmaids and/or matrons of honour'. We will make the assumption, however, that if there are two or more bridesmaids/matrons of honour, only one (the chief bridesmaid) will speak, on behalf of herself and the others – though, as we have suggested for two or more best men (see page 10), the bridesmaids could make a joint speech.

Various orders of speeches are possible. If the bridesmaid is going to reply to the toast that the groom has proposed, she may speak immediately after the bridegroom's speech, and therefore before the best man. Alternatively, the best man can follow the bridegroom, as is usual, but comment in his speech that he won't be replying on behalf of the bridesmaid because she has chosen to reply on her own behalf. If the bride speaks after the bridegroom and *she* proposes the toast to the bridesmaid, then the bridesmaid's speech will follow *her* speech. Or you may opt for some other order.

As with the bride, since the bridesmaid's speech is not one of the traditional wedding speeches, there are no rules or customs to dictate what she should say. There is no need for a long speech, and in fact since yours may be the fifth of the afternoon, it is best to be brief, though you may include some information about your relationship with the bride, how you came to be friends (unless of course you are sisters or cousins). You may include an anecdote or two about the bride, and like the bridegroom you may mention something about how the bride and groom met, how you knew it was serious, something the bride told you about the groom, and so on. Perhaps an anecdote about the wedding preparations, but make sure that no one else is going to have told the same story already. You probably do not propose a toast, but you should of course express your good wishes for the future happiness of the newly-weds.

A sample speech

[Address the audience]
Ladies and gentlemen,

[Opener, and response to the groom's toast]
It is, I know, quite contrary to tradition for the bridesmaid to speak on her own behalf at a wedding, and I know Chris would have done the job perfectly well for me. At least he hasn't got any tales to tell about me and my past! But I wanted to thank John personally for his kind words earlier this evening.

[Congratulations to the newly-weds]
I also wanted the opportunity to add my own best wishes to Julie and John for a long and happy marriage. I know I was a little unsure about John when Julie first told me about him, but in my defence I have to say that that was before I met him. I only had to see John and Julie together for the first time to know that they were made for each other. They are perfectly matched in temperament and in interests – and from their first meeting on the bus, it's quite clear that John's head fits perfectly onto Julie's shoulder! I do hope he has stopped dribbling, though.

[Remarks about the bride]
As Julie has said, we have been best friends since the day we started school together, so I suppose I probably know more about her than most people here, perhaps more even than her mum and dad. In fact

Julie knows I know things about her that her mum and dad don't know, and by the look on her face I can see that she is desperately hoping that things stay that way. I do have some tales to tell, though! For example, there was the day she was supposed to be on a geography field trip but she missed the bus, and somehow the teachers thought she was in school and the school thought she was on the trip, and she actually spent the whole day in town, shopping. Well, window shopping, because she didn't have any money with her apart from her bus fare home, and you couldn't get much in Miss Selfridge for fifty pence even in those days. And I don't suppose Julie's ever told her parents about the time we . . . and I'm certainly not going to today, because my mum and dad are sitting over there and they don't know the story either! But if the rest of you want a laugh and can keep a secret, ask me later.

[Finale]
Well, I think I have said all I need to say, so I'll stop here. I know I'm the last speaker, and I can see the DJ has arrived and is setting up his equipment for the evening, so . . . let's party!

Is it necessary to acknowledge the male-dominated tradition?

Both the above speeches begin by acknowledging that by tradition the men (bridegroom and best man) speak on behalf of the women (bride and bridesmaid). Perhaps it is not necessary for both speakers to do so, and perhaps nowadays it is not necessary for even one of them to do so. So, the bride's speech could simply begin at the second sentence:

Anyone who knows me knows that I can talk for Britain, but I'll try not to talk for too long this afternoon, though there are so many things I would love to tell you about my wonderful new husband that I could be on my feet for an hour or more!

And the bridesmaid's speech could begin differently too:

Since Chris has told us quite a few interesting stories about John's past, it would be quite unfair if Julie got off scot-free this evening. And since, as Julie has told you, we've known each other for a very long time now, it obviously falls to me to fill you all in on a few details of her past life that perhaps even John doesn't know about.

But first of all, I want to thank John for his kind words about me earlier this evening, and to take this opportunity to add my own best wishes to Julie and John for a long and happy marriage.

11 Other speakers

The bride's mother

Let's consider some circumstances in which the mother of the bride might make a speech.

Firstly, she might stand in for her husband if, for whatever reason, he is not present or not able to speak. In such a case her speech would be of essentially the same format as the father-of-the-bride speech outlined in chapter seven.

Secondly, if someone else is standing in for the father of the bride, such as an uncle or a close family friend, the bride's mother might feel that she should nevertheless say something on behalf of her husband (perhaps her late husband) and herself. She may simply want to thank the speaker for agreeing to perform this duty, or she may want to say a few more words about her husband, perhaps something very personal that no one else could talk about.

Thirdly, even if the bride's father has delivered his speech, the bride's mother may want to say a few words from a mother's point of view. If the bride's father has concluded his speech with a few words of advice to the bridegroom, she may like to end hers with a few words of advice to her daughter:

> *My husband gave some man-to-man advice to John, and I want to finish my speech with a few words of advice to Julie. This is something I found recently in a book I was reading: 'For a successful marriage, a woman has to fall in love many times – but always with the same man!' Julie, I have never stopped falling in love with your*

father, over and over again, and I hope that in the years ahead, you and John will never stop falling in love with each other. Whether you are twenty-five, fifty-five, or eighty-five, every day will be the first day of the rest of your life together, so never take each other for granted and never let your love grow cold.

The father or mother of the groom

If the father of the groom makes a speech, it will be shorter than that made by the father of the bride.

The main function of this speech will be to welcome the bride into her new family, with a few suitable compliments, and perhaps a short anecdote, and to thank the bride's father for his welcome and kind words, which he will reciprocate. He should thank the bride's father for the reception, and may add his own compliments to the caterers. And he will of course add his congratulations and good wishes to the bride and groom.

Since it is not one of the three traditional wedding speeches, there is no toast closely associated with the father of the groom's speech, but he may take the opportunity to pay compliments to his wife and to the bride's mother (and to any other of the ladies present whom it would be diplomatic to pick out for special mention), and perhaps ask the men to join him in a toast to 'the ladies':

> *Now the focus of our attention today, and rightly so, has been on two lovely girls, Julie and Emma. But I want to speak now about two other lovely girls, the mother of the bride and the mother of the groom, Mary and my dear wife Joyce. What can I say about them? Well, I do think I should at least say something about the hats, don't you? Aren't they sensational? As I said to Joyce when she showed me the hat she had bought for the wedding, the last time I saw such a spectacular array of pink feathers, it was on a flock of flamingos! And Dave admitted to me earlier this afternoon that when he first saw Mary's wedding hat, it reminded him of Carmen Miranda, but he didn't dare say so. Oops! Sorry, Dave.*

But seriously, gentlemen, look around you, at our mothers, wives, daughters and granddaughters. Are we not surrounded by beauty this afternoon? And would we not be remiss if we didn't take this opportunity of acknowledging it? So I would like to ask all of the men here to join me now in a toast to the ladies. They gladden our hearts, they delight our eyes, and we love them all dearly.

Gentlemen, the ladies!

The son or daughter of the bride or groom

When the bride and/or the groom have children from a previous marriage, one or more of the children may want to say a few words to express what their parent's marriage means to them. Normally this would happen only if the child was into his or her teens or older, but even a younger child might want to say something on an occasion which is as important and life-changing to them as it is to the bride and groom.

This could be a short speech from the bride's son:

Ladies and gentlemen,

I really don't want to talk for very long, but I wouldn't want this afternoon to pass without saying something about Michael and what he has come to mean to Shirley and me.

It's six years now since Dad died, and obviously we still miss him and think about him a lot. In a real sense he's still part of our family, and always will be. But Shirley and I knew that sooner or later we would be leaving home, and we always hoped that Mum would find someone else to share her life with. We even sent in her name and her particulars – without her knowing – to one of those online dating agencies, but we didn't much like the look of the men who replied to 'her' box number, so we ditched that plan again very quickly.

And then one day, Mum found Michael. Or he found her. Or they found each other. I don't know. You've already heard the story this afternoon. They both joined the Swing Singers on the same night, and – oh, I know this is corny, but – they've been making beautiful music together ever since.

Of course, no one can replace Dad, and Michael isn't Dad. Dad and Mum were absolutely right for each other, but Michael and Mum are right for each other too. It's just a different sort of 'rightness', their own rightness. And in the same way, though Michael can never be 'Dad' to Shirley and me, and I know he would never try to replace Dad in our lives, there is a 'rightness' in our relationship too. We have always felt comfortable with him, from the very first day we met him, and we want him to know, today in particular, that we really do welcome him into our family and that he has a special place in our hearts. Michael, we love you.

Quick reference 1
Quotations and one-liners

Love

All you need is love.
Beatles' song title.

Love means never having to say you're sorry.
Love Story film script.

Real love is a pilgrimage.
Anita Brookner, English writer.

Love is the wisdom of the fool and the folly of the wise.
Samuel Johnson, English writer.

Love conquers all things except poverty and toothache.
Mae West, American actress.

Love is like a precious plant. You can't just accept it and leave it in the cupboard or just think it's going to get on by itself. You've got to keep watering it. You've got to really look after it and nurture it.
John Lennon, English singer-songwriter.

Love is insanity.
Marilyn French, American author.

Love does not consist in gazing at each other but in looking outward together in the same direction.
Antoine de Saint-Exupéry, French writer.

Come live with me, and be my love,
And we will all the pleasures prove.
Christopher Marlowe, English poet.

Love is an act of endless forgiveness, a tender look which becomes
a habit.
Peter Ustinov, British actor.

A man has only one escape from his old self: to see a different self –
in the mirror of some woman's eyes.
Clare Boothe Luce, American writer.

For a marriage to have any chance, every day at least six things should
go unsaid.
Jill Craigie, British writer.

No woman ever falls in love with a man unless she has a better opinion
of him than he deserves.
E. W. Howe, American writer.

But to see her was to love her,
Love but her, and love for ever.
Robert Burns, Scottish poet.

Love is composed of a single soul inhabiting two bodies.
Aristotle, Greek philosopher.

Love is like the measles; we all have to go through it.
Jerome K. Jerome, British writer.

Love is the strange bewilderment which overtakes one person on
account of another person.
James Thurber and E. B. White, American writers.

Love's like the measles – all the worse when it comes late in life.
Douglas Jerrold, British humorist.

If ever a man opens a car door for a woman, it's because he has either a
new woman or a new car.
Neil Boyd, English writer.

What on earth is this love that upsets everybody, and how does it differ from insanity?
W. S. Gilbert, English writer of comic operas.

Love is a many-splendoured thing.
Title of book by Han Suyin, Chinese novelist; also a song.

There is no instinct like that of the heart.
Lord Byron, British poet.

Love must be as much a light as it is a flame.
Henry David Thoreau, American writer.

Marriage

Love and marriage, love and marriage
Go together like a horse and carriage.
Sammy Cahn, American songwriter.

Marriage is popular because it combines the maximum of temptation with the maximum of opportunity.
George Bernard Shaw, Irish playwright.

Like fingerprints, all marriages are different.
George Bernard Shaw, Irish playwright.

A successful marriage is an edifice that must be rebuilt every day.
Andre Maurois, French author.

Chains do not hold a marriage together. It is threads, hundreds of tiny threads which sew people together through the years. That is what makes a marriage last – more than passion or even sex!
Simone Signoret, French actress.

Marriage is one long conversation, chequered by disputes.
Robert Louis Stevenson, Scottish writer.

One should not think too much about it when marrying or taking pills.
Dutch proverb.

A good marriage is one which allows for change and growth in the individuals and in the way they express their love.
Pearl Buck, American author.

A happy marriage is still the greatest treasure within the gift of fortune.
Eden Phillpotts, English writer.

Marriage is not all bed and breakfast.
R. Coulson.

A successful marriage requires falling in love many times, always with the same person.
Mignon McLaughlin, American writer.

Two souls with but a single thought,
Two hearts that beat as one.
Baron von Munch-Bellinghausen, Austrian dramatist.

Marriages are made in heaven and consummated on earth.
John Lyly, English playwright.

To stay married should clearly be recognised as one of the fine arts.
Eric Linklater, Scottish author.

In every marriage more than a week old, there are grounds for divorce. The trick is to find, and continue to find, grounds for marriage.
Robert Anderson, American economist.

Marriage is a sort of friendship recognised by the police.
Robert Louis Stevenson, Scottish author.

It is woman's business to get married as soon as possible, and a man's to keep unmarried as long as he can.
George Bernard Shaw, Irish playwright.

You can't reason with men. You've just to train 'em.
Philip King, British playwright.

All married women should make a habit of saying, 'In spite of everything, dear, I'm still devoted to you.'
Eric Linklater, Scottish author.

The critical period in matrimony is breakfast time.
A. P. Herbert, English writer.

Familiarity breeds contentment.
George Ade, American humorist.

Women are all keen on marrying men they don't like much.
Kingsley Amis, English novelist.

It is a truth universally acknowledged, that a single man in possession of a good fortune must be in want of a wife.
Jane Austen, English novelist.

Next to being married, a girl likes to be crossed in love a little now and then.
Jane Austen, English novelist.

Every man expects his marriage to be different, and it's naturally a shock to find it's like everybody else's.
Basil Boothroyd, English journalist and broadcaster.

The perfect husband is one who can see his wife's faults, correct them if they need correcting, and show her what she is doing wrong.
Art Buchwald, American journalist. (He is, of course, being ironic!)

A lover and a husband are not the same. You run after somebody you want to overtake; but when you have caught him up you settle down quietly beside him. You don't continue shouting and waving.
Jerome K. Jerome, British writer.

It's easier to choose a cricket bat than pick a wife.
Michael Parkinson, British broadcaster and journalist.

Matrimony is not reputed to be invariably a bed of roses, but there is no reason why it should be a cactus-hedge.
Hugh Munro, British journalist.

Marriage resembles a pair of shears, so joined that they cannot be separated, often moving in opposite directions, yet always punishing anyone who comes between them.
Sydney Smith, British author.

Whoso findeth a wife findeth a good thing.
Bible, Proverbs 18:22.

Marriage halves our griefs, doubles our joys, and quadruples our expenses.
G. K. Chesterton, English writer.

When marrying, ask yourself this question: do you believe that you will be able to converse well with this person into your old age? Everything else in marriage is transitory.
Friedrich Nietzsche, German philosopher.

Marriage (the negative side)

Marriage is like life in this respect – that it is a field of battle, and not a bed of roses.
Robert Louis Stevenson, Scottish novelist.

Once you are married, there is nothing left for you, not even suicide, but to be good.
Robert Louis Stevenson, Scottish novelist.

Marriage is like a cage; one sees the birds outside desperate to get in, and those inside equally desperate to get out.
Michel de Montaigne, French Writer.

Marriage is at best a dangerous experiment.
Thomas Peacock, English novelist.

A man in love is incomplete until he has married – then he's finished.
Zsa Zsa Gabor, American actress.

Courtship is to marriage as a very witty prologue is to a very dull play.
William Congreve, English playwright.

A dentist got married to a manicurist. They fought tooth and nail.
Tommy Cooper, English comedian.

Strange to say what delight we married people have to see these poor fools decoyed into our condition.
Samuel Pepys, English writer.

If it were not for the presents, an elopement would be preferable to a wedding.
George Ade, American humorist.

Marriage is the most advanced form of warfare in the modern world.
Malcolm Bradbury, English novelist.

Any man who is married can appreciate why we have named our hurricanes after women.
Art Buchwald, American journalist.

Married in haste, we may repent at leisure.
William Congreve, English playwright.

Though marriage makes man and wife one flesh, it leaves 'em still two fools.
William Congreve, English playwright.

I believe in tying the marriage knot, as long as it's round the woman's neck.
W. C. Fields, American comedian.

They say that in America marriage counts as reasonable grounds for divorce.
W. Douglas Home, British dramatist.

Marriage has many pains, but celibacy has no pleasures.
Samuel Johnson, English writer.

Husbands and wives

All any woman asks of her husband is that he love her and obey all her commandments.
John Raper, American writer.

A man's friend likes him but leaves him as he is: his wife loves him and is always trying to turn him into somebody else.
G. K. Chesterton, English writer.

Let the wife make the husband glad to come home, and let him make her sorry to see him leave.
Martin Luther, German priest.

Wives are young men's mistresses; companions for middle age; and old men's nurses.
Francis Bacon, English writer.

There is a lady, sweet and kind
As any lady you will find.
I've known her nearly all my life;
She is, in fact, my present wife.
Reginald Arkell, British poet.

Advice to men

Several excuses are always less convincing than one.
Aldous Huxley, British novelist.

A little inaccuracy sometimes saves tons of explanation.
Hugh Munro, British journalist.

You don't expect to take a wife shopping with you and just come out with what you went in for.
Basil Boothroyd, English journalist and broadcaster.

No married man's ever made up his mind till he's heard what his wife has got to say about it.
Somerset Maugham, English novelist.

Protestations of undying affection are never ridiculous when they are accompanied by emeralds.
Somerset Maugham, English novelist.

To keep your marriage brimming.
With love in the loving cup,
Whenever you're wrong, admit it;
Whenever you're right, shut up.
American poet Ogden Nash's advice to husbands.

The best way to remember your wife's birthday is to forget it once.
E. Joseph Cossman, American salesman.

Being a husband is a whole-time job. That is why so many husbands fail. They cannot give their entire attention to it.
Arnold Bennett, English novelist.

Advice to women

(In house-painting) 'I'd better do the narrow bits, my hand is steadier' said boastfully, is enough to wreck any marriage.
Virginia Graham, English journalist.

My mother said it was simple to keep a man; you must be a maid in the living room, a cook in the kitchen and a whore in the bedroom. I said I'd hire the other two and take care of the bedroom bit myself.
Jerry Hall, American actress and model.

Husbands are like fires. They go out when unattended.
Zsa Zsa Gabor, American actress.

No woman should marry a teetotaller.
Robert Louis Stevenson, Scottish novelist.

Whatever you may look like, marry a man your own age – as your beauty fades, so will his eyesight.
Phyllis Diller, American comedian.

Advice to both

Never let the sun go down on your anger.
Bible, Ephesians 4:6.

Never go to bed mad. Stay up and fight.
Phyllis Diller, American comedian.

Coming together is a beginning: keeping together is progress; working together is success.
Henry Ford, American businessman.

The bedroom

Laugh and the world laughs with you: snore and you sleep alone.
Anthony Burgess, English novelist.

One good turn gets most of the blankets.
Anonymous.

Honeymoons

Honeymoon – the morning after the knot before.
Anonymous.

Sex

Sex is the most fun I ever had without laughing.
Woody Allen, American actor and director.

Sex is bad for one – but it's good for two.
Anonymous.

I knew a don at Oxford who couldn't understand all the fuss about sex. He said it only took place about three times a year at the outside.
W. Douglas Home, British dramatist.

Sex is one of the nine reasons for reincarnation. The other eight are unimportant.
Henry Miller, American novelist.

Sex between a man and a woman can be wonderful – provided you get between the right man and the right woman.
Woody Allen, American actor and director.

Bridesmaids

A happy bridesmaid makes a happy bride.
Alfred, Lord Tennyson, English poet.

Speeches

An after-dinner speaker is a man who rises to the occasion and then stands too long.
Anonymous.

Make sure you have finished speaking before your audience has finished listening.
Dorothy Sarnoff, American actress.

No one ever complains about a speech being too short!
Ira Hayes, American soldier.

I do not object to people looking at their watches when I am speaking. But strongly object when they start shaking them to make certain they are still going.
Lord Birkett, British judge.

Let thy speech be short, comprehending much in few words.
Bible (Apocrypha), Ecclesiasticus 32:8.

Talk low, talk slow, and don't talk too much.
John Wayne, American actor.

After a good dinner one can forgive anybody, even one's own relations.
Oscar Wilde, Irish playwright.

Are you all sitting comfortably? If you are, shuffle about a bit, otherwise you might go to sleep.
Frank Muir, British humorist.

When a man gets up to speak, people listen, then look. When a woman gets up, people look; then, if they like what they see, they listen.
Pauline Frederick, American actress.

I feel like Zsa Zsa Gabor's fifth husband. I know what I'm supposed to do but I don't know if I can make it interesting.
Al Gore, American politician.

Quick reference 2
Jokes

Aisle, altar, hymn

Karen and Jonathon were getting married. Karen was getting terribly nervous, and was sure she'd get into a muddle at the ceremony.

'But when is it I'm supposed to say "I do"?' she kept asking her bridesmaid, Lynn.

'Look, it's simple,' said Lynn. 'All you've got to remember is that you walk up the *aisle*, and stop at the *altar*. Then everyone will sing a *hymn*. Then the ceremony begins. It's as simple as that.'

The wedding day arrived, Karen walked up the aisle on her father's arm, and stopped at the altar beside Jonathon. But he got a terrible shock when he heard her muttering to herself as she stood beside him: 'Aisle, altar, hymn. Aisle, altar, hymn.'

Cooking

There were two men sitting in a pub discussing their wives.

The first man said, 'You know, my wife adores me. She thinks so much of me that she won't hear of me helping round the house. It's great.'

'Your wife adores you?' said the second man. 'My wife idolises me. She worships me. She treats me like a god.'

'Like a god? What do you mean?'

'Well, every night at dinnertime she gives me a burnt offering.'

The cannibals

Once upon a time there were two cannibals, a father and son, who were out looking for someone to eat. They eventually found themselves on a beach and there, lying on the sand, topping up her tan, was this gorgeous blonde. I mean, eat your heart out, Pamela Anderson.

'Ooh, Dad,' said the boy. 'Look at her. I bet she'd be delicious! Let's eat her right here.'

'Oh, no, I've a much better idea, son,' said his father. 'We'll not eat her here. In fact we won't eat her at all. We'll take her home and eat your mother instead!'

The garden centre

A man was seen rushing around in a garden centre, picking plants off the shelves and putting them back again, in obvious desperation. One of the assistants went up to him and asked what he was looking for.

'Geraniums!' said the man. 'I've got to get some geraniums! Today!'

'I'm sorry, sir. We're out of geraniums at the moment,' said the girl. 'How about some chrysanthemums? They're pretty.'

'No, they'd be no use at all,' said the man dejectedly. 'It was definitely the geraniums my wife told me to water while she was away.'

Weddings in black and white

A little girl and her mother were watching a wedding.

'Mummy,' said the little girl. 'Why is the bride wearing white?'

'That's to show that she's happy on her wedding day,' said her mother.

'Mummy,' said the little girl.

'Yes, dear?' said the mother.

'Mummy, why is the man dressed in black?'

Memory

There were two men sitting in a pub.

One man said to the other: 'My wife has a terrible memory.'

'What do you mean?' said his friend. 'You mean she forgets everything?'

'No,' said the first man sadly. 'I mean she remembers everything!'

The missing husband

Two ladies were talking about their husbands.

'You know,' said one. 'I haven't seen my husband for six months now. He went out to buy some carrots one night, and he never came back.'

'What on earth did you do?' asked her friend.

'Oh, I just opened a tin of peas.'

Women

Once there was a man who was talking to God.

'God, why did you make women so beautiful?' he asked.

And God said to him, 'I did that to make you love them.'

Then the man asked, 'Well, God, why did you make them such wonderful cooks?'

And God said to him, 'Same reason. I did that to make you love them.'

The man then asked: 'But why, oh why, God, did you make women so stupid?'

'That should be obvious,' said God. 'I did that to make them love you!'

I'm married to what's-her-name

An elderly gentleman was once having dinner at the home of an even more elderly friend. Throughout the evening, when the friend spoke to his wife, he always addressed her by some term of endearment such as

My Love, Darling, Dearest, Sweetheart, and so on. The visitor was very impressed by all these tokens of affection, since the couple had been married almost seventy years.

At one point, while the wife was doing something in the kitchen, he turned to his friend and said: 'I think it's absolutely wonderful that even after being married for all this time, you still call your wife by those pet names.'

'I've no choice,' said his friend. 'I can never remember her name!'

Birthday presents

One morning, just as a man was leaving to go to work, his wife said to him, 'I bet you've forgotten what day this is.'

'Of course I haven't forgotten, dear,' said the man. 'You'll see.'

Later that morning, the doorbell rang. When the woman opened the door, there was the delivery man from the local florist's holding a dozen red roses from her husband.

At lunchtime, the bell rang again, and there was a courier at the door, with a huge box of her favourite chocolates, from her husband.

At teatime, when the husband came home, he was carrying a small box, which, when the wife opened it, she found had a pair of beautiful diamond earrings in it.

'I *told* you I hadn't forgotten what day it is,' said her husband smugly.

'You darling!' said the woman. 'First flowers, then chocolates, and then these earrings! If this is what you do to celebrate the Queen's birthday, I can't imagine what you'll give me for mine!'

Quick reference 3
Toasts

To the bride and groom

May the roof above you never fall in, and may you never fall out.

May the worst day of your future be better than the best day of your past.

May the most you wish for be the least you get.

Love one another, have many friends, and show goodwill to all.

May all your troubles be little ones!

May 'for better or worse' be for far better and never worse.

We wish you health, we wish you wealth, and we wish you a long life of love together.

Here's to love and laughter, and happily ever after.

Here's to marriage, a journey for which no map has yet been printed nor compass yet invented.

May God, the best maker of all marriages, join your hearts as one.

May you grow old on one pillow.
    Said to be an Armenian toast.

To the lamp of love – may it burn brightest in the darkest hours and never flicker in the winds of trial.

May your hands be forever clasped in friendship and your hearts joined forever in love.

Two souls with but a single thought,
Two hearts that beat as one.

Here's to the groom with bride so fair,
And here's to the bride with groom so rare!

May you live as long as you want,
And never want as long as you live.

May your troubles be few
And your blessings many.

May your voyage through life be as happy and free
As the dancing waves on the deep blue sea.

As — and — start their new life,
let us all toast the new husband and wife.

It is written: when children find true love, parents find true joy. Here's to
your joy and ours, from this day forward.

A sunbeam to warm you,
A moonbeam to charm you,
A sheltering angel
So nothing can harm you.

Here's to the bride and the bridegroom,
We'll ask their success in our prayers,
And through life's dark shadows and sunshine
That good luck may always be theirs.

May there always be work for your hands to do.
May your purse always hold a coin or two.
May the sun always shine warm on your windowpane.
May a rainbow be certain to follow each rain.
May the hand of a friend always be near you.
And may God fill your heart with gladness to cheer you.

May your troubles be less
And your blessings be more.
And nothing but happiness
Come through your door.

May God be with you and bless you.
May you see your children's children.
May you be poor in misfortune, and rich in blessings.
And may you know nothing but happiness from this day forward.

May the road rise up to meet you.
May the wind be always at your back.
May the warm rays of the sun fall upon your home
And may the hand of a friend always be near.

May green be the grass you walk on,
May blue be the skies above you,
May pure be the joys that surround you,
May true be the hearts that love you.

May the sun bring you new strength by day;
May the moon softly restore you by night.
May the rain wash away your fears
And the breeze invigorate your being.
May you, all the days of your life,
Walk gently through the world
And know its beauty.
    Said to be a Native American blessing.

Now you will feel no rain, for each will shelter the other.
Now you will feel no cold, for each will warm the other.
Now you will feel no solitude, for each will company the other.
Now you are two persons, but both will lead one life.
Go now to your dwelling to begin the days of your life together,
And may your days be good and long upon the earth.
    Said to be a Native American blessing.

May the best ye've ever seen
Be the worst ye'll ever see;
May a moose ne'er leave yer girnal [mouse; meal chest]
Wi a teardrop in his ee. [with; eye]
May ye aye keep hale and hearty [always]
Till ye're auld enough tae dee, [old; die]
And may ye aye be just as happy
As I wish ye aye tae be.

To the bride

To my wife – my bride and joy.

When we're together and when we're apart,
You're first in my thoughts and first in my heart.

A ring is round, it turns forever.
And that's how long we'll be together.

Grow old along with me!
The best is yet to be.
    Robert Browning, English poet.

Because I love you truly,
Because you love me, too,
My very greatest happiness
Is sharing life with you.

I have known many girls,
And liked not a few,
But loved only one:
I drink to you.

Here's to the prettiest,
Here's to the wittiest,
Here's to the truest of all who are true.

Here's to the neatest one,
Here's to the sweetest one,
Here's to them all in one – here's to you.

To the groom

Here's to the groom, a man who keeps his head even when he loses his heart.
To the man who has conquered the bride's heart, and her mother's.

A toast to the man who's good and kind,
A toast to the man who's true,
A toast to the man who rules my heart,
My darling, I toast you.

To the bridesmaid/s

As Keats said, a thing of beauty is a joy forever. Please join me in a toast to the beautiful bridesmaids.

Auld nature swears, the lovely dears
Her noblest work she classes, O;
Her prentice hand she tried on man,
And then she made the lasses, O.
   Robert Burns, Scottish poet.

To friends

To all our friends,
who know the worst about us but refuse to believe it!

Here's a toast to all those that we love,
Here's a toast to all those that love us,
Here's a toast to all those that love those that we love
And all those that love those that love us.

Quick reference 4
Other possible material for a speech

Guide to being a good wife:
how to look after your husband, 1950s style

(Taken, depending on who you believe, from a 1950s Women's magazine or a 1950s school home economics textbook.)

Have dinner ready. Plan ahead, even the night before, to have a delicious meal ready on time for his return. This is a way of letting him know that you have been thinking about him and are concerned about his needs. Most men are hungry when they come home and the prospect of a good meal (especially his favourite dish) is part of the warm welcome needed.

Prepare yourself. Take fifteen minutes to rest so you'll be refreshed when he arrives. Touch up your make-up, put a ribbon in your hair and be fresh-looking. He has just been with a lot of work-weary people. Be a little gay and a little more interesting for him. His boring day may need a lift and one of your duties is to provide it.

Clear away the clutter. Make one last trip through the main part of the house just before your husband arrives. Gather up schoolbooks, toys, paper etc. and then run a dust cloth over the tables.

Over the cooler months of the year you should prepare and light a fire for him to unwind by. Your husband will feel he has reached a haven of rest and order, and it will give you a lift, too. After all, catering for his comfort will provide you with immense personal satisfaction.

Prepare the children. Take a few minutes to wash their hands and faces (if they are small), comb their hair, and if necessary, change their clothes. They are little treasures and he would like to see them playing the part.

Minimise all noise. At the time of his arrival, eliminate all noise from the washer, dryer and vacuum. Try to encourage the children to be quiet.

Be happy to see him. Greet him with a warm smile and show sincerity in your desire to see him. Listen to him. You may have a dozen important things to tell him, but the moment of his arrival is not the time. Let him talk first – remember, his topics of conversation are more important than yours.

Make the evening his. Never complain if he comes home late or goes out to dinner or other places of entertainment without you. Instead try to understand his world of strain and pressure, and his very real need to be at home and relax.

Try to make sure your home is a place of peace, order and tranquillity, where your husband can renew himself in body and spirit. Don't greet him with complaints and problems. Don't complain if he's late for dinner or even if he stays out all night. Count this as minor compared to what he might have gone through that day.

Make him comfortable. Have him lean back in a comfortable chair or have him lie down in the bedroom. Have a cool or warm drink ready for him. Arrange his pillow and offer to take off his shoes. Speak in a low, soothing and pleasant voice. Don't ask him questions about his actions or question his judgement or integrity.

Remember, he is the master of the house and as such will always exercise his will with fairness and truthfulness. You have no right to question him.

A good wife always knows her place.

Rules for a Happy Marriage

1. Never both be angry at the same time.
2. Never yell at each other unless the house is on fire.
3. Remember that it takes two to make a quarrel.
4. If one of you has to win the argument, let it be the other one.
5. If you have to criticise your partner, do it lovingly.

6. Never bring up past mistakes.
7. Never go to sleep angry or with an argument unsettled.
8. When you have done something wrong, be ready to admit it and ask for your partner's forgiveness.
9. Try to say one kind or complimentary thing to your partner at least once every day.
10. Neglect the whole world rather than each other.

Quick reference 5
Graces

If anyone other than a member of the clergy is saying the grace, it is best to keep it short and simple:

Lord God,
    On this happy occasion, we give you thanks for the food we are about to share and for the friends and family gathered here with whom we will share it.
    Amen.

The grace may include a mention of the marriage or the newly-weds:

Lord God,
    On this happy occasion, we thank you for the gift of love and marriage. We ask your blessing on John and Julie as they set out in their new life together. And bless this food that we are about to share and the friends and family who are gathered here and with whom we will share it.
    Amen.

There is a traditional grace that runs like this:

Father, we thank Thee for this food,
For health and strength and all things good.
May others all these blessings share,
And hearts be grateful everywhere.

Here are two short and simple graces:

Lord,
> *Bless this food to our use*
> *and us to your service.*
> *Amen.*

For what we are about to receive
may the Lord make us truly thankful,
for Jesus Christ's sake.
> *Amen.*

If there is a Scottish connection in either of the families, or the marriage is taking place in Scotland, why not use the 'Selkirk Grace', attributed to Robert Burns? This grace exists in two versions, one in Scots and one in Standard English:

Some hae meat and canna eat,
And some wad eat that want it; [want = lack]
But we hae meat, and we can eat,
Sae let the Lord be thankit. [thankit = thanked]

Some have meat and cannot eat,
Some cannot eat that want it;
But we have meat and we can eat,
So let the Lord be thankit.

The following is another grace composed by Burns:

O Thou who kindly dost provide
For ev'ry creature's want!
We bless the God of Nature wide,
For all Thy goodness lent.
And if it please Thee, heavenly Guide,
May never worse be sent;

But, whether granted or denied,
Lord, bless us with content.

A very simple grace that could be said by a child is the following:

Thank you for the world so sweet,
Thank you for the food we eat,
Thank you for the birds that sing,
Thank you, God, for everything.
Amen.

The Internet is an excellent source of other graces, from various religious and cultural traditions. Search on <+grace +meal>, <+graces +meals>, <+grace +mealtime>, etc. For the best selection, search on the whole web, not just UK sites.

Further sources of advice and information

The following lists provide a selection of other books and some websites where you may find further useful information about making a wedding speech.

Some of the books may be available in libraries as well as in book-shops. And there are of course many more wedding-related websites.

About wedding speeches

Law, J *Perfect Readings for Weddings* London: Random House, 2007
Smith, H *Your Brilliant Wedding Speech (Essentials)* Slough: Foulsham, 2002
Jarvis, L *Wedding Speeches (Getting It Right)* Slough: Foulsham, 1993
Jeffrey, B *Wedding Speeches and Toasts* Slough: Foulsham, 1998
Bowden, J *Making the Best Man's Speech* Oxford: How To Books, 2000
Lansbury, A *Wedding Speeches & Toasts* London: Cassell Illustrated, 1988

Sources of jokes and quotations

Bloomsbury Dictionary of Quotations London: Bloomsbury Publishing, 1992
Chambers Dictionary of Modern Quotations Edinburgh: Chambers, 1993
Murray, M Mitch *Murray's One-Liners for Weddings* Slough: Foulsham, 1994
The New Penguin Dictionary of Quotations London: Penguin, 2006

The New Penguin Dictionary of Modern Quotations London: Penguin, 2003

The New Penguin Dictionary of Modern Humorous Quotations London, Penguin 2002

The Oxford Dictionary of Quotations Oxford: Oxford University Press, 2004

www.aarons-jokes.com
www.ahajokes.com
www.hitched.co.uk/jokes
www.matrimonialbank.com/jokes

(There are many other websites where you will find marriage-related jokes and quotations, though many of them seem simply to copy from each other and their material is often very similar. Do a search for 'wedding jokes', 'marriage jokes', '+wedding +jokes' etc.)

Perfect Best Man

George Davidson

All you need to know

- Do you want to make sure you're a great best man?
- Do you want to make the groom glad he chose you?
- Do you need some guidance on your role and responsibilities?

Perfect Best Man is an indispensable guide to every aspect of the best man's role. Covering everything from organising the stag night to making sure the big day runs according to plan, it walks you through exactly what you need to do and gives great advice about getting everything done with the least possible fuss. With checklists to make sure you have it all covered, troubleshooting sections for when things go wrong, and a unique chapter on choosing and organising the ushers, *Perfect Best Man* has everything you need to make sure you rise to the occasion.

The *Perfect* series is a range of practical guides that give clear and straightforward advice on everything from getting your first job to choosing your baby's name. Written by experienced authors offering tried-and-tested tips, each book contains all you need to get it right first time.

BOOKS

Perfect Readings for Weddings

Jonathan Law

All you need to make your special day perfect

- Do you want your wedding to be that little bit more special?
- Do you want to personalise the ceremony by including readings that are just right for you?
- Do you need help tracking down a traditional reading, or finding something more out of the way?

Perfect Readings for Weddings is an anthology of the best poems, prose passages and quotations about love and marriage. Including everything from familiar blessings and verses to more unusual choices, it covers every sort of reading you could wish for. With advice on how to choose readings that complement one another and tips on how to ensure that everything runs smoothly on the day, *Perfect Readings for Weddings* has everything you need to make sure the whole ceremony is both memorable and meaningful.

BOOKS

Perfect Babies' Names

Rosalind Fergusson

All you need to choose the ideal name

- Do you want help finding the perfect name?
- Are you unsure whether to go for something traditional or something more unusual?
- Do you want to know a bit more about the names you are considering?

Perfect Babies' Names is an essential resource for all parents-to-be. Taking a close look at over 3,000 names, it not only tells you each name's meaning and history, it also tells you which famous people have shared it over the years and how popular – or unpopular - it is now. With tips on how to make a shortlist and advice for avoiding unfortunate nicknames, *Perfect Babies' Names* is the ultimate one-stop guide.

BOOKS

Perfect CV

Max Eggert

All you need to get it right first time

- Are you determined to succeed in your job search?
- Do you need guidance on how to make a great first impression?
- Do you want to make sure your CV stands out?

Bestselling *Perfect CV* is essential reading for anyone who's applying for jobs. Written by a leading HR professional with years of experience, it explains what recruiters are looking for, gives practical advice about how to show yourself in your best light, and provides real-life examples to help you improve your CV. Whether you're a graduate looking to take the first step on the career ladder, or you're planning an all-important job change, *Perfect CV* will help you stand out from the competition.

BOOKS

Perfect Personality Profiles

Helen Baron

All you need to get it right first time

- Have you been asked to complete a personality questionnaire?
- Do you need guidance on the sorts of questions you'll be asked?
- Do you want to make sure you show yourself in your best light?

Perfect Personality Profiles is essential reading for anyone who needs to find out more about psychometric profiling. Including everything from helpful pointers on how to get ready to professionally constructed sample questions for you to try out at home, it walks you through every aspect of preparing for a test. Whether you're a graduate looking to take the first step on the career ladder, or you're planning an all-important job change, *Perfect Personality Profiles* has everything you need to make sure you stand out from the competition.

BOOKS

Perfect Psychometric Test Results

Joanna Moutafi and Ian Newcombe

All you need to get it right first time

- Have you been asked to sit a psychometric test?
- Do you want guidance on the sorts of questions you'll be asked?
- Do you want to make sure you perform to the best of your abilities?

Perfect Psychometric Test Results is an essential guide for anyone who wants to secure their ideal job. Written by a team from Kenexa, one of the UK's leading compilers of psychometric tests, it explains how each test works, gives helpful pointers on how to get ready, and provides professionally constructed sample questions for you to try out at home. It also contains an in-depth section on online testing – the route that more and more recruiters are choosing to take. Whether you're a graduate looking to take the first step on the career ladder, or you're planning an all-important job change, *Perfect Psychometric Test Results* has everything you need to make sure you stand out from the competition.

BOOKS

Perfect Pub Quiz

David Pickering

All you need to stage a great quiz

- Who invented the cat-flap?
- Which is the largest island in the world?
- What is tofu made of?

Perfect Pub Quiz is the ideal companion for all general knowledge nuts. Whether you're organising a quiz night in your local or you simply want to get in a bit of practice on tricky subjects, *Perfect Pub Quiz* has all the questions and answers. With topics ranging from the Roman Empire to *Little Britain* and from the Ryder Cup to Alex Rider, this easy-to-use quiz book will tax your brain and provide hours of fun.

BOOKS

Perfect Punctuation

Stephen Curtis

All you need to get it right first time

- Do you find punctuation a bit confusing?
- Are you worried that your written English might show you up?
- Do you want a simple way to brush up your skills?

Perfect Punctuation is an invaluable guide to mastering punctuation marks and improving your writing. Covering everything from semi-colons to inverted commas, it gives step-by-step guidance on how to use each mark and how to avoid common mistakes. With helpful examples of correct and incorrect usage and exercises that enable you to practise what you've learned, *Perfect Punctuation* has everything you need to ensure that you never made a mistake again.

BOOKS

**Order more titles in the *Perfect* series
from your local bookshop, or have them delivered
direct to your door by Bookpost.**

☐ Perfect Answers to Interview Questions	Max Eggert	9781905211722	£7.99
☐ Perfect Babies' Names	Rosalind Fergusson	9781905211661	£5.99
☐ Perfect Best Man	George Davidson	9781905211784	£5.99
☐ Perfect Answers to Interview Questions	Max Eggert	9781905211722	£7.99
☐ Perfect Babies' Names	Rosalind Fergusson	9781905211661	£5.99
☐ Perfect CV	Max Eggert	9781905211739	£7.99
☐ Perfect Interview	Max Eggert	9781905211746	£7.99
☐ Perfect Numerical Test Results	Joanna Moutafi and Ian Newcombe	9781905211333	£7.99
☐ Perfect Personality Profiles	Helen Baron	9781905211821	£7.99
☐ Perfect Psychometric Test Results	Joanna Moutafi and Ian Newcombe	9781905211678	£7.99
☐ Perfect Pub Quiz	David Pickering	9781905211692	£6.99
☐ Perfect Punctuation	Stephen Curtis	9781905211685	£5.99
☐ Perfect Readings for Weddings	Jonathan Law	9781905211098	£6.99

Free post and packing
Overseas customers allow £2 per paperback

Phone: 01624 677237

Post: Random House Books
c/o Bookpost, PO Box 29, Douglas, Isle of Man IM99 1BQ

Fax: 01624 670 923

email: bookshop@enterprise.net

Cheques (payable to Bookpost) and credit cards accepted

Prices and availability subject to change without notice.
Allow 28 days for delivery.
When placing your order, please state if you do not
wish to receive any additional information.

www.randomhouse.co.uk